TALKING TO TIGERS

NICK ARNOLD

ILLUSTRATED BY JANE COPE

SCHOLASTIC

To Susila, Jill and Michelle – the top tiger team

Scholastic Children's Books,
Commonwealth House, 1–19 New Oxford Street,
London WC1A 1NU, UK

A division of Scholastic Ltd
London – New York – Toronto – Sydney – Auckland
Mexico City – New Delhi – Hong Kong

Published in the UK by Scholastic Ltd, 2004

Text copyright © Nick Arnold, 2004
Illustrations copyright © Jane Cope, 2004

All rights reserved

ISBN 0 439 97741 X

Printed and bound by Nørhaven Paperback A/S, Denmark
Cover image supplied by Corbis

2 4 6 8 10 9 7 5 3 1

The right of Nick Arnold and Jane Cope to be identified as the
author and illustrator of this work has been asserted by them in accordance with the
Copyright, Designs and Patents Act, 1988.

This book is sold subject to the condition that it shall not, by way of trade or
otherwise, be lent, resold, hired out or otherwise circulated without the publisher's
prior consent in any form of binding or cover other than that in which it is
published and without a similar condition, including this condition, being imposed
on a subsequent purchaser.

CONTENTS

Calling all teachers!	5
Welcome to Ranthambhore!	8
A tiger called Twiggy	18
The secret surprise	35
The ghost tiger	44
Blood, teeth and claws	60
Dangerous dinners	81
Tigers in trouble	102
The valley of death	112
Tara's tiger letters	124

WILDWATCH — CALLING ALL TEACHERS!

ARE YOU THRILLED BY TIGERS?

If baby tigers are your purr-fect kind of animals ... Wildwatch wants to hear from you! We're after a brave teacher to get close to tigers in their forest home. Your job will be to watch a tiger cub and keep a diary.

- *Enjoy lots of tiger action*
- *Excitement and adventure guaranteed*
- *Excellent pay, plus expenses, including travel to India*
- *Discover the romance of Rajasthan*
- *Your diary will be published by Wildwatch!*

DON'T DELAY — APPLY TODAY!

I believe in fate and, looking back, I'm sure the fortune-teller was right.

"Your name is Tina," she began. Then she shook her head. "No, but it starts with a 'T', I'm sure of it."

Wow! I thought. How did she know that? Actually, my name is Tara.

"You're a restless person, a bit of a rebel. You love adventure…"

I nodded. That's just what I'm like! I'm always rushing off in search of something different, something new. The fortune-teller sounded as if she'd known me for years!

THIS IS ME

"But deep down you're a little unsure of yourself…"

I frowned. How could she know so much? Because, to be honest, at the moment I'm at a bit of a loose end. This summer I finished my teacher-training course, but I'm not sure if I really want to teach.

The old lady peered deeper into her crystal ball, gazing at a future I couldn't see…

"Your future lies in a faraway place," she murmured. "I see a forest of wild animals. You must be careful. I can see lions … no, tigers."

"Tigers!" I gasped. When the fortune-teller mentioned my favourite animal, my heart skipped a beat. What did she know about me and tigers?

"But you must beware," continued the old lady breathlessly. A shudder seemed to run right through her.

"What is it?" I cried. "What's wrong?"

The old lady shook her head, making her big, dangling, gold-hoop earrings shake too.

"It's nothing to be afraid of, dear. The ball sometimes goes blurry. It's hard for my old eyes to make out. I'm sure everything will be for the best!"

I left the fortune-teller's tent with my brain whirring at top speed. My friend Amy was waiting outside.

"So what's he like?" she smiled.

"Eh?" I said, feeling confused.

"The man you're going to marry?" prompted Amy.

"Oh no," I muttered. "It was nothing like that!"

Amy peered at my face more closely. "You look pale!" she declared. "Has anything happened?"

I shook my head. "No, I'm fine…"

But inside my heart was still a-bumping and a-thumping. I thought of the advert I had eagerly snipped from the paper the day before. The advert about watching tigers in India… And deep down I knew I wanted the job. The fortune-teller had warned me about the dangers, but it would be an adventure. And I felt sure I'd get the job. It was written in my stars… It was meant to be!

WELCOME TO RANTHAMBHORE!

January 10

I woke up to the patter of monkeys playing hopscotch on my roof. I sat up in bed and rubbed my sleepy eyes as I tried to remember what day it was. Do monkeys ever enjoy a lie-in, I wondered with a yawn?

Just then my chances of a lie-in vanished. Someone hammered at my door with a loud BANG! BANG! BANG! It was Mani, my room boy. Mani's about 12,

MANI

and he's always smiling and eager to please, even when I'm only half-awake.

"Wake-up call, Miss Tara! Time to shine and rise!" he beamed.

"But I didn't ask for a wake-up call," I groaned.

"I knock, like you tell me to. Very good knock, finest in India!" insisted Mani.

Yes, I'm in INDIA, as if you haven't guessed! To be more exact, I'm staying in a holiday hut in the garden of the Tiger Hotel near Sawai Madhopur and Mani has just made me a cup of chai — that's Indian tea. I'm 6 km from Ranthambhore National Park, one of the best places to see wild tigers.

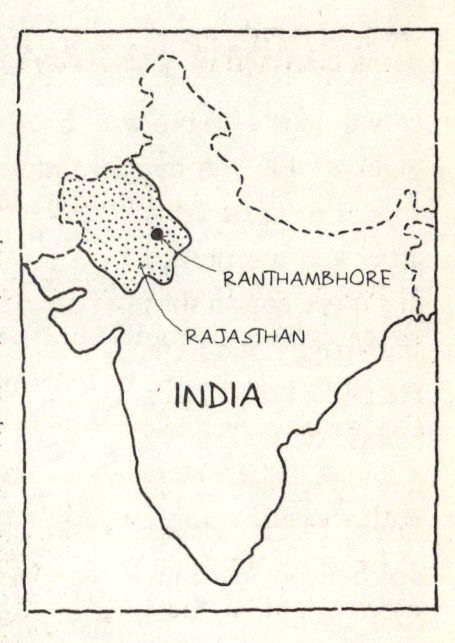

So here's the plan. I'll be watching tigers with the help of a giant-sized tiger expert named Raj. He's writing a book about the tigers in Ranthambhore and I hope he's going to be my guardian angel and tell me all about them!

January 11

Two days ago, when I arrived at Delhi International Airport I couldn't believe my eyes. Everywhere I looked there were crowds of pushing, shouting people and, all at once, my nose was full of the scent of spices and flowers and perfume. I felt swept away in an exciting whirlwind of sights and sounds and smells.

Then Raj appeared. He pushed through the crowd like a big ocean liner shoving aside small tugboats. He was huge! I only came up to his chest and I'm not that little! Raj was dressed in a loose cotton shirt and baggy trousers. He had a bushy black beard with only a few grey hairs, and thick black glasses perched on his shiny bald forehead.

"Miss Tara Bennett?" he asked politely.

"Er, yes." I stuck out my hand uncertainly.

"*Namaste*," said the giant with a gentle smile. He put his hands together and bowed his balding head.

"Mr Namaste?" I frowned. "But I'm here to meet Mr Kumar."

The giant grinned. "*Namaste* is how we greet our guests in India. I am Raj Kumar and I knew you from the photo Wildwatch sent. Please come with me."

The noise of shouting traders and yelling taxi drivers and bawling children washed over me like a sea of sound. It was all too much after my long flight to India and I began to feel very weary. I was glad Raj had offered to drive me to Ranthambhore.

Raj's car turned out to be a dusty old jeep. Foam padding spilled from its seats and its battered canvas roof was open at the sides.

"It doesn't keep off the rain but it keeps out the sun," Raj explained cheerfully. "It could do with a wash – I mostly drive it on dirt tracks."

The jeep's engine spluttered into life and, once we were clear of the smelly smoggy Delhi traffic jams, Raj showed how fast the jeep could go.

We tore along the bumpy road, past villages of mud houses and women in bright saris carrying pots on their heads. I glimpsed quiet temples and ponds and children herding goats. We whizzed past old men on creaky carts drawn by buffalo. There was just so much to see and my poor jet-lagged brain couldn't take it all in.

Sometimes mad, hooting, fist-waving drivers in battered trucks or rusty lorries would try to pull past us. And I'm sorry to say Raj would put his foot down and race them until the jeep rattled and shook and nearly took off as it flew over the bumps in the road.

Raj didn't say much during the journey, but I did find out a little about the national park.

TARA'S TIGER NOTES
RANTHAMBHORE NATIONAL PARK

1. The park is named after a ruined fortress, 1,000 years old, which stands on a huge rock overlooking the forest. The fortress once belonged to powerful kings – the maharajahs of Jaipur.

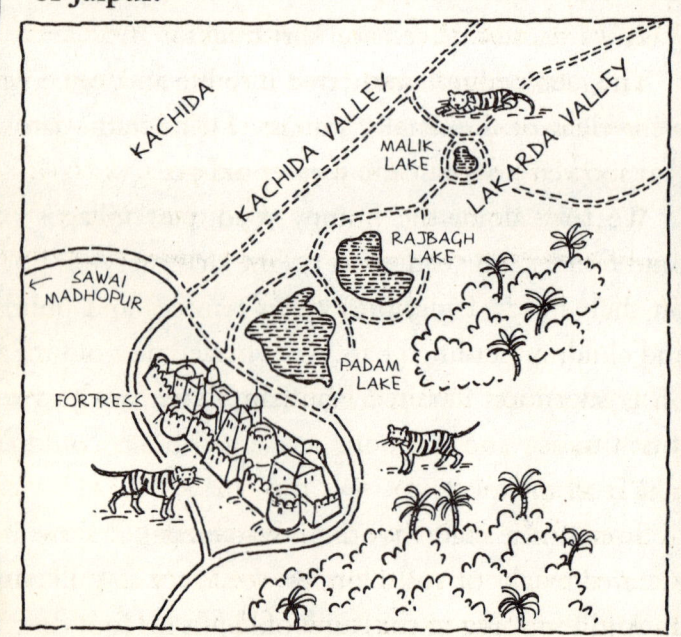

2. In the olden days, the maharajahs used to hunt tigers in the park, but anyone else who killed a tiger was chased out of the kingdom.

YOU'RE MINE – ALL MINE!

3. The park covers over 400 square kilometres. It's mostly forest but there are lakes and ruined temples built by the maharajahs long ago.

4. Experts have spotted more than 300 types of birds, and there are hundreds of monkeys and crocodiles and two types of deer – sambar and chital. If you're really lucky, you might see some of the rarer animals, such as leopards or bears ... and, of course, tigers!

January 12

This afternoon I visited Ranthambhore for the very first time.

"Don't expect to see too many tigers," Raj warned. "The tigers we'll be watching live close to the fortress. If we see them, we see them. But I think they'll be resting at this time of day."

Despite Raj's warning, my heart was pitter-pattering. Was I about to see my first ever tiger in the wild? I crossed my fingers and made a special secret wish. I was still crossing my fingers as we drew near the park.

At the end of a deep, dark valley, I saw a crumbling gateway with huge wooden doors. It looked like the entrance to an enchanted kingdom and I half-expected to see goblins guarding the gate. But instead there were two forest rangers in smart uniforms.

The two guards bowed politely and gave Raj the *Namaste* greeting.

"I have special rights," said Raj proudly. "Tourists must stick to the roads and tracks, but I can go where I please. Right now the area where our tigers live is closed to all visitors except me. That way they aren't troubled by tourists."

As we drove on, I found myself exploring a forest full of weird and wonderful trees I'd never seen before. Raj taught me some of their names. He pointed out shady jemun and ber trees. There were dhauk trees with gorgeous reddy-purple leaves and fig trees full of monkeys. I saw huge banyan trees that looked like mini-forests and thick, rustling clumps of bamboo where tigers could hide or leopards might lurk.

HI THERE!

On the other side of the Padam Lake, Raj stopped the jeep so I could enjoy the view of the fortress. It looked just like a fairytale city with its high crumbling battlements and towers and temples. I could just see myself as Princess Tara being woken by Prince Charming with a nice cup of chai.

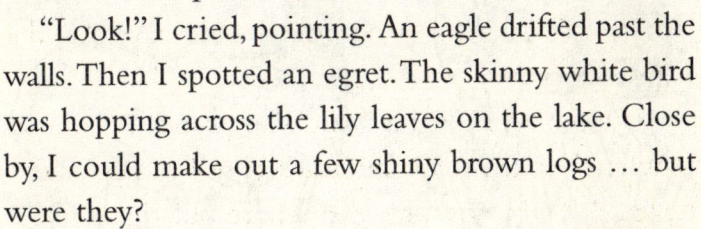

HOW CHARMING!

"Look!" I cried, pointing. An eagle drifted past the walls. Then I spotted an egret. The skinny white bird was hopping across the lily leaves on the lake. Close by, I could make out a few shiny brown logs ... but were they?

"They're mugger crocodiles," said Raj, following my gaze. "They're basking in the sun."

I made a mental note not to fall in the lake and risk getting mugged by the muggers.

CAN YOU SPOT THE CROCODILES?

Through my binoculars I could see herds of brown beasts munching the knee-high grass. They were deer, sambar and chital, a tiger's favourite prey (the animals it eats). We watched the deer and Raj patiently pointed out the differences between them...

SAMBAR: SHAGGY COAT. MALES HAVE ANTLERS. LARGER THAN THE CHITAL.

CHITAL: WHITE SPOTTY COAT. THE MALE IS DARKER AND LARGER.

Suddenly the deer scattered. "Help!" shouted the chital (or at least that's what it sounded like). "Dhank!" bellowed the sambar in reply.

"What's happening?" I cried. I was expecting a big stripy tiger to bound from the bushes.

"False alarm," said Raj calmly. "Chital aren't too clever, and they get scared by an oddly shaped log."

Well, after seeing the crocodiles, I could understand that!

We watched the deer and chatted happily until sunset. And that's when the awesome Technicolor show began. It looked as if a mad painter had gone crazy with a giant paintbox. SPLAT! He painted the fortress cliffs purply red. SQUISH! He turned the trees the colour of pink roses. SPLOT! The muddy shores of the lake shone like gold.

Suddenly the whole forest shook with sound. AOOOOOOOMMMH! AOOOOOOOMMMH! The hills and the fortress rock rang with noise. I shuddered. My heart was in my mouth. I felt half scared and half thrilled. AOOOOOOOMMMH! AOOOOOOOMMMH! It was like a huge hippo burping into a massive metal megaphone!

But Raj had a smile on his bearded face.

"Ah – a tiger," he said happily. "It sounds like Akbar. He's the top male tiger around here. I think he's talking to you, Tara. He is saying, 'WELCOME! WELCOME TO RANTHAMBHORE!'"

A TIGER CALLED TWIGGY

January 13

Last night my head was spinning with the sights and sounds of Ranthambhore. But I dropped off to sleep as easily as falling off a log, and slept like a log too! I slept so well that I found it hard to get going in the dark hour before dawn. And I wasn't ready when Raj arrived to take me to the park. Raj wasn't too happy, and I started the day in the dog house.

"Sorry," I yawned. "It's very early, isn't it?"

"Not for the tigers," said Raj sternly. "They hunt at night, so our best chance of seeing them is right now, or at sunset. We had better hurry."

Raj drove extra fast to get to the park before dawn, and we just made it. As we rumbled through the old gateway, the stars were starting to fade. A pale light glowed over the hills but it was still shiveringly cold and I was glad of my warm fleece.

Slowly, slowly, the bright-red sun squeezed its way over the black hills. The lake glimmered in a gently glowing mist and the fortress seemed to float like a cloud-castle. I looked up in wonder – was I still asleep? Could all this be a dream?

Raj stopped the jeep and pointed out a track that led through the long, golden grass towards the forest.

"I'm not promising anything," he whispered. "But the tigress often comes this way to drink."

Tigress – that's a female tiger.

I peered around nervously, in search of the stripy beast. "Er, is it safe here?" I gulped.

Raj grinned. "We'll be safe enough. You can't be too careful with tigers, but they're used to jeeps. It's one reason we had to close the area. The tigers were going too close to tourist jeeps and giving the visitors a nasty shock!"

I held my breath and tried not to fidget. After half an hour I felt colder than ever. Would we be waiting all day, I wondered?

Raj told me to be patient. "She could be here at any moment," he whispered.

As we waited, a red-and-blue kingfisher landed on a bush with a wriggling frog in its beak. The little bird bashed the frog against a branch until the frog stopped moving. The bird tried to gulp the frog down. But it had to take a break with a pair of froggy legs sticking out of its mouth.

GULP!

All at once something deep inside me, some sense I never knew I had, sparked into life. Something was coming, I felt sure of it! And then, suddenly, there it was!

Oh – it's only a dog! I thought at first. But the animal was stripy. And it was BIGGER than a dog. My mouth dropped open in a long, slow gasp. The beast seemed to glow in the golden dawn. Now it was less than 40 metres away. I could see dots and dashes and splotches and splashes of black on its whiskered face. Through my binoculars I could even make out its round golden eyes. It was the most breathtaking, the most beautiful, creature I had ever seen.

With trembling hands, I raised my camera and pressed the button. The tigress heard the tiny click. She stopped and stared. And my heart stopped with her.

MY FIRST SIGHT OF RANI

For a minute, I scarcely dared to breathe. Then the tigress padded a little closer. If Raj hadn't been with me I'd have screamed! But the tigress turned away and slipped into the long grass. Her stripy coat blended into the shadows, and she was gone.

Raj lowered his binoculars.

"That's Rani," he said. "Her name means 'queen' in Hindi."

Rani, I learnt, was Akbar's mate. She was the mother of the cubs I'd be watching.

"WOW!" I gasped. I didn't know what to say. I could have said "WHAT A BEAUTY!" or "SHE'S S-O-O SCARY!" But I was too stunned to think straight. You could have knocked me down with a feather!

TARA'S TIGER NOTES
TIGER BASICS

1. Tigers are more closely related to lordly lions than cuddly cats. Experts put tigers and lions together in a group of animals called *Panthera* or "roaring cats".

2. Tigers vary in their appearance according to where they live. For example, the tigers in Sumatra are lighter and more stripy than the biggest tigers in Siberia. But all tigers are the same type of animal or species (spee-shees).

3. Before the 1950s, wild tigers roamed central Asia and the islands of Bali and Java but human hunters killed them off.

4. Today there are only about 500 Sumatran tigers left in their natural home. And only a few thousand Asian tigers still live in the wild, mostly in Siberia and India.

Here's a map showing where tigers can be found:

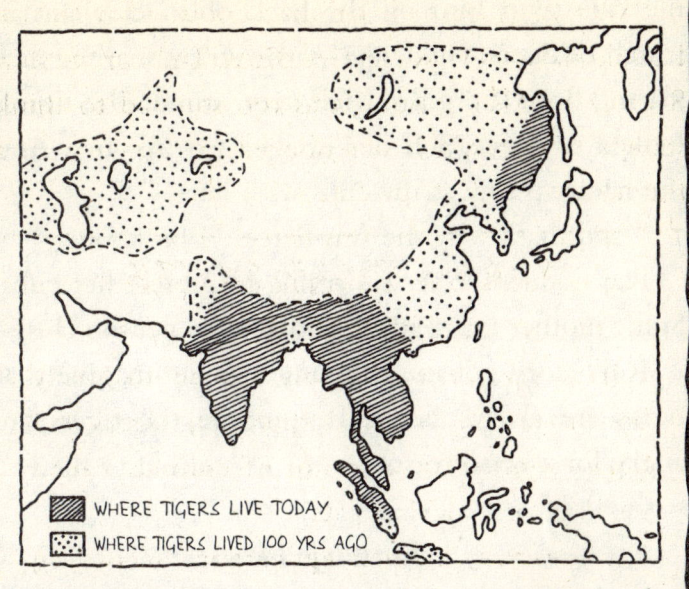

WHERE TIGERS LIVE TODAY
WHERE TIGERS LIVED 100 YRS AGO

5. Tigers live in mountains, swamps and forests. And as long as they're near water and have lots of animals to eat, they're happy cats.

After Rani's disappearing act, Raj backed the jeep up a few hundred metres.

"Rani needs to drink in peace," he explained. "But we may see her come back this way."

Rani didn't return. But while I was looking out for the tigress, Raj told me the story of the first time he saw a tiger.

"It's something you never forget," he said. "When I was a boy my father was a forest guard at Kanha, that's another national park. One day, my father let me ride with him on the back of an elephant in search of tigers. Suddenly I saw a stripy, snarling face glaring from the grass. I felt very scared. The tigress looked so fierce, and her eyes blazed like fire. And she had two tiny, stripy cubs with her—"

"And that's why she was fierce?" I broke in.

Raj nodded. "She was trying to protect her cubs. Some mother tigers attack people who get too close."

Raj's story got me thinking. People imagine that tigers are always fierce. But maybe the tigers are angry for a good reason?

January 14

"Some mother tigers attack people…"

I couldn't get Raj's words out of my head. Before I left for India, Wildwatch gave me lots of safety tips and I thought I'd better refresh my memory…

TIGER DANGERS

1. An adult tiger is strong enough to kill a human. But even though thousands of people visit the forests where tigers live, tigers don't attack humans that often.

2. Tigers hunt the animals their mums taught them to hunt, so humans aren't top of a tiger's dinner menu.

3. Most tigers are actually scared of people. They hide if they scent a human. And even a whiff of human wee will make a tiger lie low for a while.

4. If a tiger does attack, it's because...
- The human gets too close to a tiger cub. A mother tiger will kill to defend her cubs.
- The human takes a tiger by surprise. A scared or startled tiger can attack a person.
- The tiger is a man-eater. Some tigers DO hunt people, but it's often because they're starving. The tigers eat people because humans have driven away all the deer.
- The tiger makes a mistake. Some people get pounced on when they crouch down to go to the toilet. A tiger may think the squatting human is a deer.

DEAR LITTLE HUMAN

LITTLE DEER

5. So tigers can be a danger. The best advice is don't go too close to a tiger or do anything to upset it.

Well, having read the facts, I'm not scared. I love adventure and I'm sure Raj knows what he's doing. After all, he's been watching tigers for 20 years! And there wasn't any danger of being eaten by a tiger today. Raj only goes tiger-watching four days a week. On Wednesdays he takes a day off. There's not much point in watching tigers on Wednesday. It's the day crowds come to worship at the Hindu temple in the fortress. The tigers keep well away from the people.

Raj spends Thursdays and Fridays catching up with all the things he can't do when he's tiger-watching – emails and telephone calls, and writing his book on tigers. So it looks like I'll be getting three days a week to work on this diary and write letters to the folks back home.

January 16

Today I've been chilling out. Yes, I'm lying in the hotel garden, listening to my Walkman and sipping a delicious lime juice drink called *nimboo pani*.

Aw, come on! A girl needs to relax sometimes! Anyway, I could do with a rest. Tiger-watching tires me out and I need time to get used to being here. So much is new to me in Ranthambhore and my poor brain is overloaded! I'm still pinching myself to prove it's not some incredible dream!

But even in the hotel garden there are new sights to see. Today I watched the langur monkeys in the gular tree next to my hut. A gular is a type of fig tree and the bigger monkeys were merrily munching the fruit. Meanwhile the little monkeys played tag on my roof and the baby monkeys enjoyed a swing on their mums' whippy tails. I love monkeys! These ones look so cute with their grumpy little faces and smart silver hoods!

GRUMPY MONKEY

But why am I talking about monkeys? I should be telling you about tiger cubs. With a bit of luck, I'll be seeing some tomorrow!

TARA'S TIGER NOTES
TIGER CUBS

1. Most tiger cubs are born in March or February. When they're born, they're only the size of guinea pigs!

I'M BIGGER THAN YOU!

NO YOU'RE NOT!

2. Tiger cubs are brought up by their mum. Their dads don't have much to do with them.

> **When the cubs are about two, they wander off to find their own territory (that's a hunting area).**
>
> **3. But before then the tiger cubs need their mum. They can't hunt for themselves and their mum has to catch their supper.**
>
> **4. A tiger mum trains her cubs to hide while she's away. If the cubs wander off, they could end up as a tasty treat for a hungry jackal or leopard.**

January 17

What a let-down! Seven hours of searching and no tiger cubs!

"It's often this way," said Raj gloomily. "You think you know where the tigers will be and they're not there. And you wonder where they've got to."

"So where have they got to?" I wondered.

"Well, they could be anywhere," said Raj with a shrug of his big shoulders.

Anywhere and nowhere, I thought glumly.

By midday I'd had enough. I asked Raj to drop me in the old stone square below the fortress.

It was lovely sitting under the big, shady trees around the square but I badly wanted to see the fortress. So I set off up the steep zig-zag path to the top of the rock and slipped into a romantic dream. As I passed under the crumbling gates, I saw myself as a rani in a jewelled sari. Rani Tara riding up to my fortress on a big grey elephant.

For three hours I wandered spellbound around the temples and palaces and tombs. I felt I was exploring a lost world in the sky, with a surprise around every corner. A beautiful pavilion shaded by trees, a palace made of columns and domes…

A cheeky mongoose played amongst the fallen stones of a silent tomb. As I watched the quick little mongoose, with its funny pink nose and its bright brown eyes, I imagined it fighting its deadly enemy – the poisonous cobra snake. What a hero!

A MONGOOSE

Next I wandered over to the battlements and gazed at the forest. From up here the park was a sea of trees with little bumpy hills and shiny puddle lakes. And the tigers were somewhere out there. Where were they hiding, I wondered? Maybe in the thick bushes under the trees, or the long grass by the lakes. They were out there hunting and hiding, and living lives that I wanted to write about. If only I had a pair of extra-powerful X-ray specs to see them!

I bet Raj wishes he had X-ray glasses too. He looked for tigers all afternoon, without success, while I'd enjoyed a lovely time in a lost world!

January 18

I'm writing today's diary in red ink – it's how I write all the important days. Now I bet you're wondering what makes today so super-important. Well, if you'll only listen and stop asking questions, I'll tell you…

Funnily enough, things didn't start too well. I woke up hungry. My tummy gurgled like an old drain, but Mani, bless him, handed me a chapatti (Indian bread) and bananas to keep starvation at bay.

Half an hour later it still wasn't light and Raj and I were bumping along a track through the shadowy forest. Suddenly Raj turned the wheel. The jeep swerved across the track and hurtled into the forest.

Big rough-tough tree trunks loomed around us. They were the sort of trees you wouldn't want to meet on a dark night, or even a dark dawn. And I felt doubly scared because Raj had switched off the jeep's headlights!

Raj's bearded face was fixed in a crazy grin.

"Slow down, we'll have an accident!" I pleaded.

"Hmm?" said Raj. "Oh, it's not as bad as it looks!"

"It looks pretty bad to me!" I snapped.

The next moment we stopped and only my safety belt saved me from diving through the windscreen.

"We get out now," said Raj in a low voice. "But please be very quiet. Tourists aren't allowed to do this, but we tiger scientists have to!"

He put a big finger to his lips and crept over a crunchy carpet of dead leaves. Still shaking from my near-death experience with the trees, I tottered after him. Again, I found myself wondering if this was completely safe. But Raj had a plan. And all I could do was follow him and feel amazed that such a big man could move so silently.

TIPPY-TOE

"Now we wait," Raj whispered. He waved his hand as a signal for me to crouch in the leaves.

And so we waited ... and waited ... and waited some more. I'm not sure how long we were crouching in the forest because I was still half-asleep, but it was long enough for the first sunny rays of dawn to splash among the leaves. And still we waited...

All at once I felt an odd prickling feeling at the back of my neck. A sense of breathless excitement came over me. Oh-er, I thought, it's my secret tiger sense again! But was I right?

Yes! Suddenly Rani slipped from the shadows like a film star. But this time she wasn't alone. WOW – there they were! Two stripy cubs. The little tigers were only the size of my granddad's dogs.

"Oooh!" I gave a little cry of excitement and quickly snapped their picture.

RANI AND HER CUBS

The cubs hadn't spotted us, even if their mum had. One scrambled onto Rani's back. I guess that was out of order because she waved him down with her soft, stripy paw.

Meanwhile the other cub was setting off on an adventure. A BIG adventure for a tiger cub. She wobbled along a fallen tree trunk, carefully placing one paw in front of the other. Halfway along, she rubbed her furry face against a twig and chewed the leaves. The sunlight gleamed on her white chin and glistened on her whiskers. I could just imagine her calling to her mum: "Look at me, I'm a tightrope walker!"

And what a little star she was! She had bright golden eyes and pale patches on her cheeks. She was thinner than her brother and her front legs were less stripy.

"I know," I said. "I'll call her Twiggy. She's skinny, and she plays with twigs. Look! She's even got a little 'T' marking on her cheek — that's T for Twiggy!"

"Twiggy?" said Raj lowering his binoculars and giving me a funny look. Then he shrugged. "Well, call her what you like! I've been calling her 'R3'."

"Arthree?" I said. "Is that an Indian name?"

Raj put his hand over his mouth to muffle his laughter. "No," he chuckled. "It's a code! R stands for Rani. Three means she was the third cub I saw."

"You mean Rani has another cub?" I asked excitedly.

Raj shook his head sadly. "There was another boy cub, but he died. Tigers often have three cubs, but it's rare for all of them to make it."

Meanwhile my eyes were still glued to Twiggy and her brother. My brain had been taking in every stripe and whisker. I felt sure I'd know them again!

Twiggy tumbled off her tree trunk and scampered back to her mum and brother. It was time to go. Rani stretched and yawned and led her cubs away into the forest.

"Well," said Raj after the tigers had disappeared, "you haven't told me what you're calling Twiggy's brother."

"Oh, that's easy!" I smiled. "He's Prince!"

Raj stroked his beard as he thought about the name. "That's good!" he chuckled. "A prince is a rani's son. And may I ask which cub you will write about?"

I didn't need to think about my answer...

"Why, Twiggy of course!"

HI, I'M PRINCE

It's been a great day. I've seen the cubs and I've given them names. And do you know something? I think Raj likes my names, because by the end of the day he was using them too!

THE SECRET SURPRISE

January 20

Two days have passed without a sniff of tiger. I know tigers are hard to find but this is BOR-RING! Are they training for a Hiding From Humans Competition?

So instead of watching tigers, I found myself watching Raj…

The Raj is a large, rather shy, creature. His favourite food is bananas and he is good at walking fast along forest tracks. In fact he's so fast that I have to trot to keep up with him.

The Raj likes to relax with a well-thumbed book of poems. But he didn't get much of a chance today because I pestered him with questions about tiger-tracking. After our failed tiger searches I wanted to know how anyone ever finds them!

TOP TIGER-TRACKING TIPS

1. Some experts use special equipment to track tigers. A radio collar sends out signals, which tell the expert where a tiger is. To put the collar on safely, the expert needs to fire a tranquillizer dart at the tiger to send it to sleep. Other experts set up automatic cameras to snap a tiger's picture as it passes by.

2. Another way to tell if a tiger's about is to listen for monkey and deer calls. Monkeys and deer are animal pals. Deer warn their monkey mates if they sniff a tiger and the monkeys tell their four-legged friends if they spot a tiger from their tree. The tiger must feel pretty unpopular at times - especially when birds join in the alarm-call chorus!

3. Tiger paw marks (or pug marks, as the experts call them) offer lots of clues about the tiger that made them...

- Male pug marks are wider, larger and less pointy than a female's.

FEMALE   MALE

- The depth of the pug mark shows how heavy the tiger is.

> - The spacing between the prints shows whether the tiger is strolling or hurrying.
>
> STROLLING TIGER
>
> TIGER IN A HURRY
>
> - An expert can sometimes tell which tiger made a paw print from the shape of the pug mark.

And to prove it, Raj showed me Rani's pug mark. He can tell it belongs to Rani because the front left toe print points away from the other toes. But this afternoon we came across another set of tracks. Raj crouched down to match the mark against a set of cards. Then he measured the pug mark just to make sure.

"Ah," he said happily. "I thought so – Akbar's been this way."

I gazed along the line of pug marks and spotted a lumpy, brown pile. *Was it? Could it be?*

"Yes, they're tiger droppings," said Raj cheerfully. "They're dry and old. Full of useful clues, though. Tigers swallow hair from the animals they eat. The hair tells us about the tiger's supper."

I peered at the smelly pile and shuddered. And I spent the rest of the afternoon trying not to think of Raj rummaging through a pile of tiger poop.

January 24

Dawn at Ranthambhore. The sky was a glaring yellow and the clouds glowed pinky-red as Raj gazed at the body of a deer that Rani had caught last night. He peered through his binoculars and then scribbled in his notebook. The deer lay on its side in a clearing. I won't go into the grisly details, but the manky meat wasn't my idea of a breakfast treat.

I shivered. The air was clear and cold, and there were frosty silver trails on the grass. I stamped my feet and blew on my hands to keep warm. Hurry up, Raj, I thought.

Raj shut his notebook.

"See how the deer hasn't been hidden!" he said. His breath steamed in the cold air. "That means Rani is most likely keeping watch close by. She'll be back when she gets hungry. We'd best keep our distance!"

A couple of crows landed on the body and began to peck at the flesh. But maybe they knew Rani was around because they flapped off to eat their beakfuls of meat in safety.

It was cold waiting for Rani to show up. I shivered and my fingers went numb. I felt as if I was slowly turning to ice.

Suddenly Raj patted my arm. There was Rani, standing by the deer! Peering through my binoculars, I saw her stripy tail swishing from side to side as she sniffed the body. Then she began to tear meat from the bloody bones. But not for long. A moment later, she stopped in mid-mouthful. She had spotted us!

SHE'S SPOTTED US!

Rani glared in our direction and gave an angry hiss. "What are you looking at?" she seemed to snarl.

Tigers hate being bothered at breakfast (or any other mealtime). I held my breath. Would Rani run at us? No, it was just a gentle warning! Raj touched my arm and made a tiny movement of his hand to point us back the way we'd come. Slowly and silently, we crept away like a pair of meek little mice.

"It's odd," I said to Raj when we reached the jeep, "but when Rani hissed, I felt as if she was talking to us."

I expected Raj to laugh and tell me not to be silly, but instead he nodded slowly.

"Yes, it's very strange, I often feel that the tigers are talking to me. And I talk back to them. It's all in my head of course!"

"So it's a bit like having tigers on the brain!" I joked.

"Yes, maybe so. I know I've been mad on tigers for years!" laughed Raj.

January 25

Today there was even less meat on the deer. Last night someone had made a massive meal of it.

"Probably Rani and the cubs," said Raj.

But another tiger had scented the deer. And all at once this tiger walked boldly from the forest. He was a male and his coat shone a bright brilliant orange. At the sight of him, I felt a tingle in my fingertips. This tiger was even bigger than Rani. He had bigger muscles and his head and paws were massive!

The big male tiger padded over to the deer with his head held high and his coat rippling with every step. He stuck his huge head into the bushes and sniffed the body. *Mmm!* he seemed to think. A nice half-eaten sambar deer steak. And it's not *too* manky! He took a great greedy bite of the flesh and fed hungrily for a few minutes. At last, when he'd eaten enough, the male tiger yawned and stretched then padded into the bushes.

I looked at Raj. "Is that—?" I began.

Raj nodded. "Yes, you've just seen Twiggy's father."

January 26

Notice anything? I keep telling you that tigers are massive but then I forget to say how big they are! Well, we didn't get to see any tigers today, so I decided to write some notes about tiger size…

HOW BIG IS A TIGER?

1. Male Indian tigers can be almost 3 metres long and females can be over 2.5 metres. (These lengths include about 80 cm of stripy tail.)

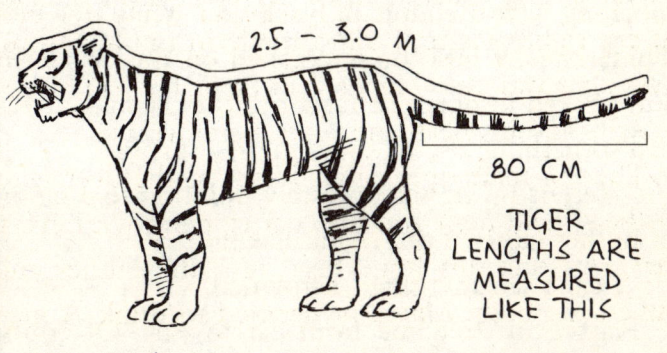

2.5 – 3.0 M

80 CM

TIGER LENGTHS ARE MEASURED LIKE THIS

2. A tiger's forearm can be half a metre long.
3. A tiger's fearsome fangs can be nearly 13 cm long!

Why not use a tape measure to take your own body measurements? I measured Mani and compared him to a tiger.

"I feel most tiny, Miss Tara," he said with a shudder. "I am hoping that I never get to greet a tiger on a dark night!"

I agreed. I wouldn't want to go too close to a tiger and I guess you wouldn't either!

January 27

This morning all that was left of the deer was a pile of bones and a few raggedy tatters of flesh. The tigers had scoffed all they could and Raj reckons that vultures and jackals have gobbled the rest.

I guess the tigers won't be back, and all we saw all morning were a couple of black-and-white tree pies. These cheeky little birds perched on the deer's ribs and pecked hungrily at tatty titbits of flesh. But Raj had something else to show me – a surprise.

"Here it is," he said, proudly pointing to a clump of bushes close to the Malik Lake.

"I can't see anything," I frowned.

Raj's grin stretched from ear to ear. "Of course you can't see it, that's the whole point."

"But if I can't see it, why are you showing it to me?" I said hotly. I felt grumpy at not seeing a tiger.

"It's hidden!" laughed Raj. "That's the surprise — it's a hide, a secret place for watching tigers!"

I peered more closely at the thorny bushes. Ah yes! I could just make out a screen made of grass.

"Can I look inside?" I asked.

"Of course. Be my guest," said Raj with a bow.

The hide was a big box, so cleverly hidden that it was hard to see against the forest. Inside there was a mattress and a container for food. It looked snug and comfy, and I was just admiring it when Raj sprang his second surprise on me.

"I am planning a night-time tiger-watch when Rani's next around. Perhaps you would like to come too?"

I looked at Raj and then at the hide. "Um — OK!" I said bravely. It sounded quite an adventure. But then I pictured myself in a dark forest full of hungry tigers. "Er — just so long as it's safe," I added.

"Oh yes, it's plenty safe," said Raj soothingly. "I designed it myself. The thorns stop the tigers from getting too close."

THE GHOST TIGER

February 1

This morning we saw the tiger family resting just a few hundred metres from the hide.

"Rani will hunt in this area tonight and we could see some action from the hide," said Raj excitedly.

I felt a nervy buzz of excitement as I packed my bag for the night ahead…

```
THINGS TO TAKE FOR A NIGHT
      OF TIGER-WATCHING
Bananas and chapattis (watching tigers is hungry work)
Warm clothes
Water to drink, but nothing sweet (ants will drop
by to share any sweet drinks)
```

> Anti-mosquito spray (there's sure to be a few biting blighters)
> Binoculars
> Night glasses
> This diary and a pencil
> Notebook
> Torch
> Camera and camera stand

As the sun went down, Raj and I knelt on the saggy mattress and peered through the eye-holes in the hide. We had an eye-popping view. The sunset glowed red and orange and gold, and the lake shone like a mirror of melted metal. The whole scene looked so lovely, I wished I could hang it on my wall!

I was still admiring the sunset when Raj patted my arm. "Look, a wild boar!" he said.

THIRSTY BOAR

The boar was a tough-looking character with a bristly mane and curved tusks. I felt glad he couldn't see us. He trotted down to the lake and stuck his snout in the water with a wet slurping, slobbering sound.

No sooner had the boar left when a group of chital crept from the forest. The deer were edgy and listened for tigers. HOOOO! an owl called softly. The chital froze and gave the owl a worried look. The owl stared back at them like a stern teacher.

SCARED DEER

The chital were right to feel nervous… "HELP!" cried one in alarm. The deer scattered as Rani stalked into view with the cubs toddling at her heels.

As the forest grew dark, the tiger family wandered down to the lake for their evening drink. Rani drank for a long time, lapping water like a cat. The cubs were less thirsty and soon they began to play. Round and round in circles they ran, each trying to bite the other's tail. Then Rani called them with a grunt, and the tiger family slipped back into the forest.

As the last daylight faded, a peahen picked her way to the lake. The bird had seen the tigers and she was nervous. Scared, she took a sip of water and scuttled away. Next, a family of monkeys dropped by for a bedtime drink. The granny monkey gazed in disgust at the mud churned by the deers' hooves.

"WHAT A MESS. THOSE DEER HAVE NO MANNERS!" I imagined her complaining.

The monkeys made their way to the lake, taking care not to walk in the muddy bits.

Through the night glasses, I spotted a sambar deer and her baby. The mother deer sniffed the air to check no tigers were lurking nearby. The coast was clear and she made her way to the water's edge. Then she weed into the lake ... and drank from it!

Sambar often do this. I'm sure the granny monkey would be most offended. The thought of her grumpy face gave me the giggles. I giggled so much that I had to put down the night glasses.

THOSE DEER ARE BEHAVING LIKE ANIMALS!

"May I take a look?" asked Raj.

Raj doesn't have night glasses and he's been itching to get his hands on them. Hmm – I bet that's one reason why he set up tonight's tiger-watch!

I peered out of the hide. Everything was black. It was like trying to see with your eyes shut. It took time for my eyes to see by the dim light of the stars.

DHANK! The deer called out in alarm. A moment later I heard the deer and her baby dash into the forest. The bushes rustled as the chital made a quick getaway. What was going on? My hands shook. I felt sure there was something out there. Something big. My secret sense told me it had to be a tiger!

Yes – there it was! I could just make out a ghostly tiger shape heading towards the lake.

Raj was gripping the night glasses tightly.

"I-I don't believe it. It's old Half-fang!" he gasped.

"Half-fang?" I repeated. I could tell from Raj's voice that this tiger wasn't good news. I watched tensely as the tiger glided along the lake shore and vanished into the night.

Raj switched on his dim torch and scribbled something in his notebook.

"I'd know Half-fang anywhere. He's got a broken tooth and a twisted paw from a poacher's trap."

"Poacher's trap?" I asked. Wildwatch had told me something about poachers. They're people who break the law to kill tigers…

Raj rubbed his eyes and yawned. "The park bosses do try to protect the tigers but poaching has been a problem at Ranthambhore for years," he said sadly. And with that, the tired tiger expert told me about poachers.

TARA'S TIGER NOTES
TIGER POACHING

1. Even after tiger hunting was banned in 1970, hundreds of tigers have been killed by poachers. Many poachers are local people who use traps and poisons to kill tigers. They sell the skin and body parts to rich dealers.

2. The beautiful tiger skins are made into rugs. The body parts are used to make traditional oriental medicines...

• Tiger bones are supposed to heal diseases of the joints.

• Tiger blood is said to make you healthy.

• Tiger tails are believed to cure skin diseases.

• Tiger eyeballs are thought to cure some types of fainting fits.

But all of these so-called cures are useless!

As I listened, I felt I needed matchsticks to prop my eyes open.

"You look worn out," said Raj. "Maybe you should sleep for a bit. I don't think we'll be seeing Rani tonight."

My eyes were already shut and the next thing I knew, it was dawn. An orange mist covered the lake and the water glittered with light. I felt cold and cramped and my teeth chattered like castanets.

I was still half-asleep when Raj patted my arm. "Wake up, Tara," he urged. "Akbar's here!"

Akbar was standing by the lake. His whiskers twitched and his eyes were bright and fierce. Slowly, he sniffed the ground.

"He's scenting Half-fang," whispered Raj.

Akbar wasn't a happy tiger. His ears were flat, and his black lips curled in a snarl. Then he stalked off into the bushes with his long tail thwacking crossly from side to side.

I decided to ask Raj more about Half-fang when I was less tired. Just then I could feel my comfy bed calling me…

February 3

Imagine you're a monkey. You're in a tree near Padam Lake, happily munching fruit when something horrible happens … you're terrified by a tiger cub!

That was the scene we came across this afternoon and Twiggy was the cub in question. She had climbed into a tree and the monkeys were cackling their alarm calls at the tops of their voices. But why were the monkeys so miffed? As usual, Raj had the answers…

TARA'S TIGER NOTES
TIGERS AND MONKEYS

1. Monkeys are scared of tigers for the very good reason that tigers make a meal of monkeys.

2. Tigers attack monkeys on the ground but adult tigers are too heavy to climb trees. Cubs climb trees, but they're not skilful enough to hunt yet.

3. Sometimes a tiger roars under the monkeys' tree. The roar gives the monkeys such a fright that some of them fall off their perch into the tiger's open jaws. It's a tiger fast-food takeaway!

I LOVE FAST FOOD!

Twiggy gazed at the monkeys in wide-eyed wonder. She couldn't understand what the fuss was about. So she jumped onto a lower branch and thought it over, with her stripy tail swinging from side to side.

That gave Prince a mean idea. He sneaked up on his sister and made a grab for her tail. He missed and Twiggy hissed. But Prince wasn't going to take the insult lying down and leapt onto the branch. A cat fight looked on the cards until Rani gave a soft growl.

WHEEEE!

"COME DOWN AT ONCE!" she seemed to snap.

The two little cubs leapt off the branch and raced over to their mum. Tiger cubs always do what they're told, unlike the young humans I came across during my teaching practice!

Rani had decided to lead the cubs to the lake, but the cubs couldn't walk in a straight line. They wanted to scamper in all directions and explore interesting clumps of grass. Then they played a game called "I can jump further than you!" When the tigers were a safe distance away, Raj beckoned me to follow him.

"Where are they going?" I whispered as we crept after the tigers.

Raj put his finger to his lips. "Sssh!"

I got the message, and we soon found out…

Rani was paddling! The lake looked chilly but the mother tiger looked as happy as a kid at the seaside. How could she? I thought with a shiver.

"COME IN, KIDS, THE WATER'S LOVELY!" I imagined Rani calling. But the cubs huddled on the muddy bank. They didn't look too keen on a dip.

I remembered what Raj had told me last week. How he "talks" to tigers in his head…

"I don't blame you," I silently told the cubs. "That water looks cold enough to freeze your whiskers off!"

Rani huffed crossly. She splashed out of the lake and grabbed Prince in her jaws. Returning to the water she dunked his stripy bottom in the muddy lake. Prince squealed but he sat still as his mum gave Twiggy the cold-water treatment.

TIGER SWIMMING LESSON

Raj laughed. "It's a swimming lesson! Tigers love water. They enjoy cooling themselves in it."

"But it's not exactly cooling-off weather!" I protested.

"Got to learn some time!" laughed Raj. "Hey look! Rani's backing into the water. Tigers don't like getting their faces wet."

Rani might have odd ideas about teaching swimming, but she's still a good mum. As if to prove it she brought Twiggy and Prince back to the bank. She licked the mud off the cubs and let them rub her face with their wet noses.

LET'S RUB NOSES

Afterwards the tiger family snuggled up for a feed of milk. Oh well, I guess swimming is hungry work!

February 7

My diary has led a boring life these last few days. Untouched by human hands, it's been sitting on the desk while I've been busy groaning in bed. Yes, I'm ill. I'm not a whining whinge-bag but I really am suffering! I'm not going into the dreadful details, but Wildwatch did warn me not to touch the water in India. And so did my mum…

"It's full of germs, dear," she worried.

"How would you know?" I said cheekily. "You've never been to India!"

"But you hear the most dreadful stories. Oh, do be careful, Tara!"

Well, Mum, I've tried to be careful. I always drink bottled water. I even brush my teeth with the stuff. But this week I ruined everything! Like a forgetful fool, I forgot that germs live in ice. And I let Mani put ice in my drinks…

OUCH! It feels like an iron fist is squeezing my guts! I'm shivering and I feel as weak as a day-old tiger kitten. I've been like this for two dreadful days, and as for my too-frequent trips to the toilet … the less said the better! When I first came to India, it was like a beautiful dream. Everything was new and strange. But now I've had enough. I wish I was at home! But I'm too ill to go anywhere … except the toilet.

February 8

OK, so maybe I don't want to go home. This morning I felt well enough to sit up in bed and chat to Raj. He brought me a box of gooey Indian sweets and a bunch of flowers, bless him! To be honest I'm not up to eating, but it was a nice thought and Mani enjoyed the sweets.

SCOFF MUNCH!

"I hope you are feeling better soon!" said Raj kindly.

"We are all hoping that Miss Tara will be right like the rain very soon!" agreed Mani, his mouth full of sweets.

"I feel a lot better already, thank you!" I whispered weakly.

I wasn't fooling anyone. We all know I won't be up to tiger-watching for a few days. But at least I can write again and Raj says I ought to say a few words about Twiggy's early life.

"Imagine you're Twiggy and tell your readers about what happened before you arrived," he suggested. Mani passed me my diary and I began to scribble Twiggy's story…

Twiggy's tiger tale

Hi! My name's Twiggy and I'm a tiger cub. I was born in September at the end of the monsoon rains. I'm only five months old, but I'm a clever girl, and I've written my whole life story. It's even got the bit before I was born!

My mum is called Rani and my dad is Akbar – but I don't see too much of him. Mum and Dad got together after Mum called to Dad with a cry of "Aooch Aooch!" I don't know what Dad saw in Mum, but I guess it wasn't her singing!

AOOCH, AOOCH!

After a few days, Dad wandered off and left Mum all alone until me and my brothers were born. Mum had us in a sheltered place where no one could find us. When we were born, Mum let us find our way to her tummy to feed. How did we do it? I'll never know because we couldn't see a thing!

We were blind for two days and even after that everything was all blurry and fuzzy for a couple of weeks. But at last we saw Mum and each other for the very first time. It was the biggest thrill of my life!

> *A couple of days later my little brother got lost and that was the last we saw of him. But me and my other brother, Prince, were OK. Mum fed us on milk and licked us clean when we were dirty, and we grew three times bigger in our first month.*
>
> *When we are naughty, Mum will growl and slap us to make us good. But if anyone tries to hurt us, Mum will kill them, and she's well up to it! But sometimes even Mum gets scared. She opens her big toothy mouth and grabs us up behind our heads and carries us to a safer place.*
>
> DON'T LET GO, MUM
>
> YUK!
>
> *A couple of months ago, Mum started bringing meat for our tea. I thought this stringy, messy stuff was vile but I like it now. So does Prince. He's always after my share. Huh – typical greedy boy!*

"Very good!" laughed Raj, pretending to clap his hands together. "I must say I'm glad Twiggy wrote her story for your diary because I never saw the cubs when they were younger. Rani must have hidden them too well!"

February 11

I'm in a BAD mood! Raj has just brought me the double dose of bad news.

People in the villages around Ranthambhore are talking about a skin dealer. They say he's offering 10,000 rupees for a dead tiger. No one seems to know any more, but Raj is worried that someone will go after our tigers.

"And that's not all," added Raj. "Half-fang is still around. My ranger friend, Govinder Singh, saw him near Padam Lake yesterday."

"What?" I said, sitting up in bed and spilling my cup of chai. "I thought he was just passing through. What's he up to?"

Raj shook his head. "I wish I knew. Half-fang was chased out of his territory by a younger tiger. He's moved into Rani's territory and he could be a danger to the cubs."

"What do you mean?" I asked as my dicky stomach started to whoosh like a waterfall.

Raj looked even more unhappy. "If he took over Akbar's territory, he could kill the cubs. You see, that's what male tigers do…"

BLOOD, TEETH AND CLAWS

February 12

When Raj told me the cubs were in danger, I pestered the poor man to check on them.

"Please, Raj," I begged. "You can work on your book another day!"

Raj sighed. "OK, if it puts your mind at rest," he agreed.

"Thank you," I said, giving him my most dazzling smile.

So today Raj went looking for the cubs, but he didn't find a thing. Not even a pug mark. And now I feel even worse! Where are the tigers? Have they been caught by poachers? Have they been attacked by Half-fang? What's going on? Oh boy – do I hate mysteries! And I feel so helpless…

February 13

I'm sitting in bed reading this diary and sipping *nimboo pani* with salt and sugar and definitely NO ICE! Oh dear, why can't I ever be organized? The day before yesterday I said that Half-fang had been kicked out of his territory, but I forgot to tell you why territories are so important!

TARA'S TIGER NOTES
TIGER TERRITORIES

1. Imagine you live in the garden! Now imagine all the kids in your road live in their gardens and you share the same dad. Can you picture that? That's what tiger territories are like! Tiger mums have 15-30 square kilometres (that's some garden!) and tiger dads can roam up to 300 square kilometres.

2. Tigers have to do loads of walking. And to get about, they have a sort of tiger motorway – a network of paths and tracks and dried-up streams.

3. But a tiger doesn't have its territory to itself. Other tigers pass through in search of their own territories. Some are young tigers (males travel further than females), and some are old tigers that have lost their territories.

4. Tigers need territories to live in and find food. A tiger without a territory has a hard life. They can starve or risk a fatal fight with another tiger.

5. Tigers can put up with visitors, especially if there are a lot of deer to hunt. They can even share killed animals – a sort of tiger dinner party. But if the newcomer stays too long or tries to take over, well, that's when you get fights.

After I finished my tiger notes I lay in bed and wondered what was happening to my tiger family. Lots of things could have taken place while I lay ill. Rani and Akbar might be putting up with Half-fang hanging about. Or maybe Half-fang could have taken over Akbar's territory...

Were the cubs OK?

The question niggled away like an itch I couldn't scratch. I just had to take action, so I told Raj I'd be up to tiger-watching tomorrow. Raj saw the determined look on my face and he didn't argue.

We agreed Raj would pick me up at 5 am and we'd go looking for the cubs! I'm glad I'm doing something at last. And I really, really hope that tomorrow brings better news!

February 14

This morning I found myself staring at a dead deer in the blood-red dawn. The body was covered in leaves and I felt like a cop at a crime scene. "Yes, I figure it's a murder," I wanted to say. "What do you think, Detective Raj?"

Meanwhile, Raj was rubbing his big bristly beard. "I've found a pug mark. I think it's Rani…"

"Then she's OK! There's been no trouble with Half-fang?"

"It doesn't look like it," agreed Raj. "If we wait here we might see Rani turn up to eat. We could even see the cubs."

We waited for an hour but Rani didn't show up. And with no Rani to chase them away, a whole queue of forest animals came to eat the deer instead.

First in line were a couple of jackals. They sniffed out the body in the leaves and began to nip at the flesh. Then they were spotted by a crowd of quarrelsome vultures...

HUNGRY JACKALS AND VULTURES

THUMP! WHUMP! CRUMP! The vultures landed and shooed away the jackals. Then they began to rip and strip the meat from the bones, and gulp and gobble grisly lumps of flesh. More of their vulture pals turned up, shoving and pushing and screeching. I don't think vultures know the meaning of manners.

"Rani won't like this," Raj frowned.

TARA'S TIGER NOTES
TIGERS AND VULTURES

1. For the tigers, it's bad enough when vultures steal their suppers. But the vultures also poo on the tigers' food. Not surprisingly,

that puts the tigers off eating it! Would you fancy a hamburger with a pile of vulture poop on top?

BUZZZZZ

2. Sometimes a tiger gets so cross that it kills a vulture, but the tiger won't touch the bird's body. Tigers seem to hate the taste of vulture as much as their poop!

3. Hunting is hard work and if a tiger loses its meal, it will have to hunt all over again. If the tiger can't catch anything this time, it will be tired and hungry and risks growing weaker and starving. So the vultures are putting a tiger's life on the line. No wonder tigers hate vultures!

But where were the tigers? Raj said they would turn up to feed, but we waited for three whole hours without seeing a whisker. So what's going on? Not even Mr Tiger Expert Raj Kumar can say!

February 15

Dawn near Malik Lake. We were following a line of Rani's pug marks through the icy, frosty grass. I was looking at the ground and that's how I found it. An ugly metal thing lying at my feet in the crisp, dead leaves.

"What's this?" I called to Raj.

Raj came over and knelt down to take a closer look. He frowned and his worry lines deepened. "Oh no!" he groaned. "It looks like a poacher's trap!"

"A trap?" I stared at the thing in horror.

"Someone must have left it there expecting Rani to come back this way."

The trap was a dirty, rusty snare designed to catch a tiger's leg. It looked strong enough to hold the tiger in terrible pain until the poacher came to beat it to death.

HELP!

I shuddered as I pictured Rani caught and crying in this terrible thing. "Why can't people leave tigers alone?!" I burst out.

Raj carefully dug around the trap with his hands, clawing at the cold earth with his nails. When the trap was loose, he used the point of a stick to shut it with a harsh, metal snap. Then he gingerly picked up the trap and placed it in the back of the jeep. With all thoughts of watching tigers gone, we raced back to the fortress square to find a ranger.

February 16

When he saw the trap, the park director was deeply shocked. He doubled the number of forest rangers at the park gates and ordered extra patrols both night and day. Let's hope they keep the poachers away!

But as I often ask, where are the tigers? Again, we looked everywhere without success. Soon I began to fret and fidget. Terrible thoughts of poachers and Half-fang fluttered around in my head like mad moths.

But Raj told me not to worry. "I think the tigers are lying low," he said. "They'll be trying to hide from the rangers, and each other."

"To avoid fights?" I asked, brightening up.

Raj nodded. "The tigers tell each other where they are, so they don't meet up."

"But how do they do that?" I asked, thinking of our tiring, tigerless drive today. If only the tigers could tell us where they were!

TARA'S TIGER NOTES
TIGER MESSAGES

1. A tiger can't go anywhere without leaving an I WAS HERE message. Special glands on the tiger's toes, face, tail and bottom make a scent that gets rubbed onto bushes or leaves as the tiger passes by.

2. Tigers wee on certain trees or bushes. No, they're not being disgusting! The smelly wee tells other tigers whether the tiger is male or female and whether a tigress is ready to mate. The wee stays smelly for several days and even humans notice the strong smell.

3. Tigers leave piles of poop lying about. They're smelly KEEP OUT! signs for other tigers. And stop making faces! For a tiger this feels as natural as you sending a text message.

4. Trees can be tiger signposts too. Tigers scratch the bark to show other tigers how big and strong they are. Higher claw marks show a big, scary tiger stretched up to make them!

HEH HEH — THIS'LL FOOL THEM!

February 17

Pheeeeuuuuw! Hear that? It's me breathing a BIG sigh of relief! Today we found the tiger family and they're as right as rain. Clearly there's been no bust-up with Half-fang so far!

Rani was snoozing in the long grass near Padam Lake. She was lying on her back with her legs in the air and we could see her black-and-white stripy tummy. Judging by Rani's bulging belly, she'd just made a meal of the mangled deer nearby. The cubs were full up too, and enjoying a half-hearted sleepy wrestling match.

Meanwhile, a group of vultures gathered in a tree in the hope of stealing another free lunch. The vultures hungrily craned their scrawny necks and eyed up the meat. I imagined them deciding what to do next…

"The vultures are wise birds," said Raj. "They know that Rani can wake at any second. Tigers never sleep deeply."

LOOK AT THAT LOVELY MEAT!

YES, BUT LOOK AT THAT TIGER!

But one vulture was willing to risk a run-in with Rani. The smallest vulture flapped down and pecked at the deer. Rani didn't stir, so the others followed. Soon they were all stuffing their beaks. Rani rolled on her side. She opened one eye and then the other. She lifted her head. Her eyes narrowed in fury. Silently and smoothly she raised her big shoulders … and a second later she charged.

With a heart-stopping "ROARRRR!" Rani bounded towards the birds. WHACK! SWAT!

SWIPE! She walloped the vultures with her paws. The vultures screeched and squawked and flapped their wings until the feathers flew. But somehow they got away. And maybe they've learnt a lesson – *you don't tangle with a tiger*!

After the vultures had flown off, Rani decided to hide her dinner. She grabbed the deer's body in her jaws and dragged it backwards into the bushes. She made it look easy, but Raj whispered that it would take six men to shift that weight. I bet they couldn't do it with their teeth, though!

February 21

Akbar is stressed to his amber eyeballs and I'll give you one guess what's keeping him up at night. It's big, it's stripy, it's vicious and its name begins with H.

Yesterday Half-fang was spotted near the Jogi Mahal. (The Jogi Mahal is the lovely forest rest house just below the fortress rock.) Raj heard the news from Govinder and stopped by to tell me the shocking story.

"A cook saw Half-fang walk past the kitchen," said Raj. "The tiger acted as if he owned the place. The cook was very scared – he had never seen a tiger so close! He jumped in the air and dropped his pots and pans with a big crash. Govinder says there was a lot of roaring in the forest last night."

AOOOOOOOMMMH! AOOOOOOOMMMH! I imagined the two big male tigers warning each other.

"KEEP OUT! BACK OFF! I'M THE TOP CAT AROUND HERE!"

"NOT ANY MORE, PAL!"

And I thought of poor little Twiggy and Prince snuggling up to their mum in terror.

February 22

Tiger-watching is full of surprises. You can trek for days without seeing one and then you trip over *four* without even looking! We were driving past the Rajbagh Lake and, for once, we weren't looking for tigers. We were after a dead deer that Govinder had spotted. Raj wanted to search the area for pug marks. That's when we came across the tiger family ... and we were in for a big surprise.

Rani was lying in the grass watching her cubs play nearby, but the tigers weren't alone. There was another tiger, sitting in the shallow water like a stripy lake monster.

I felt myself grow tense. "OH NO! Not Half-fang?!" I groaned.

Raj and I grabbed our binoculars and sighed with relief at exactly the same moment. It was Akbar! For once the tiger dad was spending some quality time with his kids.

"Fascinating," murmured Raj. "It's rare, but tiger fathers *can* get together with their families..." Happily, he scribbled the details in his notebook.

I couldn't take my eyes off the tigers. I'd never seen anything like this, and even Raj doesn't see four tigers too often. Together we watched in awe-struck silence.

After about 20 minutes, Akbar pulled himself to his feet and splashed back to the shore. Then, without a second glance at his family, he padded away into the long grass.

Meanwhile, Twiggy and Prince were still playing peacefully. Well, maybe peacefully isn't the word! The cubs were wrestling and chasing and leaping on each other. I wondered what they thought about Akbar. Did they recognize their dad? If only they could talk and tell us!

THE TIGER FAMILY

February 23

Talking tigers. It sounded such an exciting idea that I decided to find out about tiger language. And what's more they do have a sort of "language"...

TARA'S GUIDE TO TIGER "TALK"

1. Purring. If you want to know why a cat purrs, try giving her some fresh fish! Tigers don't purr much, but I bet they can purr louder than your happy kitty!

MY PURR IS LOUDER THAN YOURS!

2. Prusten. Try making a sort of huffing through your nose. That's the sound a tiger makes to say "hello" to a friend. If you make this sound to a tiger, you ought to rub cheeks with it - that's a tiger kiss! On second thoughts, don't try it - it's a bit dangerous!

3. Ah ah! That's the cry that the cubs make to their mum. Isn't it cute? And she'll often call to them with a sort of cough or grunt.

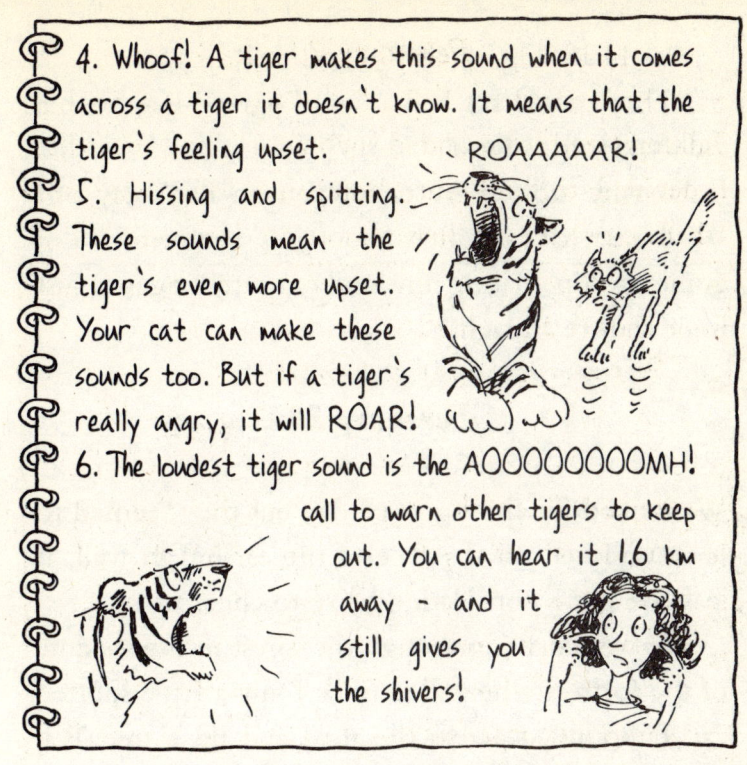

> 4. Whoof! A tiger makes this sound when it comes across a tiger it doesn't know. It means that the tiger's feeling upset.
> 5. Hissing and spitting. These sounds mean the tiger's even more upset. Your cat can make these sounds too. But if a tiger's really angry, it will ROAR!
> 6. The loudest tiger sound is the AOOOOOOOOMH! call to warn other tigers to keep out. You can hear it 1.6 km away – and it still gives you the shivers!

As I finished off my tiger guide I drifted into a lovely daydream. I saw myself as an expert tiger interpreter who could explain every sound tigers make. It would be dead brilliant and I bet I'd get my own TV show!

February 27

I'm afraid I've got some BAD NEWS. Akbar is badly hurt. Govinder only got a quick look, but he's definitely limping and he's got a nasty gash in his side. When I heard the news, my insides seemed to leap off a cliff.

"It's Half-fang, isn't it?" I said to Raj.

"They must have had a fight!" agreed Raj, with a sad shake of his head.

So why did it have to happen on Raj's day off? We'll just have to find the tigers tomorrow! I'm going to stop writing now and cross my fingers. I just hope they're all right!

February 28

We looked for the tigers all day but they seemed to have vanished off the face of the earth. Oh well, at least we got a consolation prize to cheer us up.

We were driving though the forest in the shadow of the fortress when all at once I saw a large spotted cat. It bounded across the road and up a tree. Raj braked and we peered at the tree through our binoculars. Yes, we could see the gleam of its bright eyes. There was no doubt, we were looking at a leopard! Quickly, I grabbed my camera and took this piccy.

LOOK, A LEOPARD!

The leopard didn't move as it gazed back at us. It was only a few seconds, but it seemed to last for ever. At last the leopard crept down from the tree and disappeared into the forest.

Raj was grinning like a lottery winner. "Well, that was a surprise!" he exclaimed. "Leopards mostly hunt at night and hide from tigers. That's the first one I've seen in over a year!"

March 1

We were following a new set of tiger tracks. Well, new for me. Big, ugly pug marks with one paw twisted to the left. Half-fang's trail. But the track led to more than we'd bargained for...

There ahead of us, and no more than 30 metres away, was Rani. Her tail was swiftly swinging, her head was lowered and her ears were sticking up. Rani was listening hard, the very picture of a tensed-up tigress. But what was the matter?

ARE YOU FOLLOWING ME?

Raj took my arm and we began to back away.

"Where are the cubs?" I whispered softly.

"Hidden," Raj hissed, "maybe in the grass—"

Suddenly the grass rustled and parted and Half-fang stalked into the open. My heart was in my mouth. I nearly jumped out of my skin.

The old tiger's eyes were narrow and mean. His whiskers stuck out like live wires. He snarled and treated us to a sight of his ugly yellow fangs, including the broken one that gave him his name.

ANGRY HALF-FANG

Rani's eyes were big and dark and fearful, her muscles tight and tense. But she couldn't run away. "HISSSSS!" she spat at Half-fang. "BACK OFF FROM MY CUBS OR YOU DIE!"

But the big male was playing it cool, acting as if nothing was wrong. Maybe he wasn't bothered and maybe he was. Rani took a silent, slow-motion step towards him. He was half as big as her again, but she had to save her cubs...

Half-fang growled, low and angrily. Rani growled back, trying to guess his next move. Suddenly everything happened too fast to see. The tigers were up on their hind legs, boxing, scratching, hissing, spitting. Springing and spinning around each other like deadly dancers. Biting and clawing and slashing ... this was a giant catfight with killer cats...

Who was going to win? I wanted to ask Raj, but I didn't dare speak. I could only watch in stunned silence.

THE TIGER FIGHT

Suddenly the fight stopped! It was as if an invisible referee had rung a bell! Just like that, the two tigers sat down and glared evil tiger stares at each other. Half-fang had a scratched and bleeding nose, but Rani had a big, raw wound in her side. I gasped. The ripped and torn skin made me shudder.

"Rani's hurt!" I cried.

I couldn't bear to watch and I closed my eyes – but then I peeped through my fingers. Half-fang stood up. He growled and crashed into a bush. He snatched something brown and floppy, and stalked away with it.

It was a baby deer. Perhaps it was Rani's breakfast. So that's what Half-fang had been after! I could feel my rage rising. Half-fang had hurt Rani. He'd hurt her just to steal a free snack! How could he? I wanted to snatch a stone and chuck it at Half-fang. I wanted to punch his big bleeding nose! I clenched my fists and ground my teeth. "Ah ah!" I could hear Twiggy and Prince crying in the long grass. If Rani was too badly hurt to hunt, her cubs would starve. And Akbar had been missing for three days. Even if he was still alive he'd be in no shape to save the cubs from Half-fang. Hot, angry tears flooded down my cheeks. My cubs could die ... and there was nothing, nothing, I could do to save them!

DANGEROUS DINNERS

March 2

Yesterday, we watched Rani limp painfully away into the long grass in search of her cubs.

"We'd better not follow," said Raj. "Rani's hurt and she's not in the best of moods."

"But we've got to!" I protested. "We've got to take a closer look at that wound!"

Raj shook his head firmly. "It's just not safe," he warned.

"But the cubs are in danger and we need to keep an eye on them!" I said. I blew my nose and dashed the tears from my eyes. Raj could see I wouldn't take "no" for an answer.

"OK," he said. "We'll look for them tomorrow when things have settled down a little."

I reached up and gave him a quick hug. "You're a very kind tiger expert!" I sniffed.

"Steady on! We might not find them!" said Raj.

Well, that was yesterday. Today we drove through an empty forest without seeing any sign of tigers. My mind conjured up terrible thoughts. What if we came across a dead Rani with flies buzzing around her? But, thankfully, Rani was still alive.

"Oh that looks sore!" said Raj gazing at the red, raw wound.

I sucked in my breath and shuddered. It's terrifying what a tiger's claws can do. But at least the wound wasn't as deep as we feared. Raj thinks it will heal in a few days.

"As long as she stays out of fights," he added grimly.

And Rani did stay out of trouble. We spent the whole afternoon watching her lying by Malik Lake. She licked her wounded side as the cubs played nearby.

"It's the best thing," said Raj. "Tiger spit contains a natural germ-killer. It will do her lots of good."

I looked at Rani as she painfully licked her wound, and hoped the tiger spit would do its stuff.

Later

Good news! Half-fang has been spotted by some tourists at the Semli waterhole. I heard them chatting at the hotel. They got the shock of their lives when the fierce old tiger stepped across their path! I asked them to tell me the whole story and when they'd finished, I nearly hugged them! If Half-fang's at the Semli waterhole, he must be safely out of Rani's territory.

March 3

More good news – Akbar is found! We were following his pug marks by Malik Lake when the tiger stepped from the bushes and sat down in our path!

I stopped and stared.

"You can see he's been in a fight," said Raj. "Look at that torn ear and that nasty scratch on his nose."

"He hasn't got a gash, though," I said.

"No, thank goodness!" said Raj. "Akbar got off lightly. Half-fang could have killed him."

I felt like cheering but I knew I had to keep my mouth shut. It doesn't do to upset a tiger!

HURRAH – AKBAR'S OK!

Oh well, I think I'll have a little cheer now!

After eyeing us up for a few moments, Akbar got to his feet and padded our way. I looked at Raj nervously, expecting a signal to back off. But Raj was reading Akbar's mood. The male tiger was laid-back, his ears were up and his tail gently curling. So Raj decided it was safe to stay still.

"Don't be angry," I said to Akbar in my head. "We know you're hurt and we just want to see you're OK."

Akbar sniffed a bush. He stuck out his big pink tongue and made a screwed-up tiger face. Then he turned and gave the bush a quick squirt of wee.

"What was that face?" I asked as we watched Akbar slip into the forest.

"Flehmen," replied Raj. "Tigers always make that face when they sniff a spraying place."

Well, fancy that! As I said, tigers sniff wee to find out useful info – but imagine every time you got a text message you had to wrinkle up your nose and stick out your tongue! Why not practise making this face in the mirror? Just make sure you don't do it at your teacher ... or a passing tiger!

GRRR!

March 6

Today Raj dropped by for a cup of chai and a spot of gossip.

"The people of the village are still muttering about the mystery tiger-skin dealer," he told me. "They say he's very rich. He owns many cars and a big house in Delhi."

"So who is he, and why don't the police arrest him?" I asked.

Raj shrugged. "No one knows his name and there's no hard proof of anything. India is full of gossip and stories."

More questions. More mysteries. So what's the truth? Is the skin dealer just a story, or something more sinister? And who left the tiger trap? That was real enough!

March 7

I'm writing today in red ink but it's nothing to do with tigers... It's to do with me!

After a long day of failing to find tigers, Raj halted the jeep near Malik Lake so we could watch the sunset. As the red sun slipped behind the dark hills, I breathed in the delightful perfume of sweet leaves and wild honey.

The scent was heavenly! It was so relaxing that I wanted to sniff it for ever! If only I could bottle it, I'd make a fortune!

TARA'S FOREST PERFUME $1000 a sniff

"It's beautiful here," I murmured to Raj who was standing beside me.

"Mmm, I've always thought so," Raj replied.

And that's when I knew…

"I think I belong here," I said. "I'm not a visitor anymore."

"You certainly seem at home," agreed Raj.

But it's more than that, I thought. In my heart of hearts I knew I was falling in love. Falling in love with Ranthambhore. Falling in love with India. I'm not looking forward to leaving next month. I want to live here … always.

March 8

Today Rani really put her life at risk! It all happened on the banks of Rajbagh Lake. Recently the days have been hot. The sun blazes from an empty blue sky and hairdryer-hot winds blow dust in my eyes. The sambar have taken to hanging out by the lake to find water, but this evening we found out that Rani has followed the deer. And she's hunting by day…

Raj spotted Rani before the deer noticed her. "She's left the cubs, and she's getting ready to charge," he whispered.

I followed his pointing finger and glimpsed a stripy head in the long, waving grass.

One of the sambar stags stopped and sniffed the air. He was a huge animal with antlers as long as my arms. Instantly Rani stood statue-still. The big male deer stared towards the tigress. He couldn't see her, and the evening breeze blew her scent away from him.

Rani crouched lower in the grass and watched as the stag led the other deer towards the water. Step by stealthy step, the tigress inched forwards on her belly. And step by silly step, the deer walked towards danger.

We crept forward until I could see Rani more clearly. Now I could see her eager ears twitching and her strong leg muscles tensing up. Her sore side looked much better.

Just then Rani tore from the grass like a stripy firecracker. In one, two, three giant bounds, Rani reached the deer. The gap between supper and starvation, death or escape, was measured in heartbeats. The sambar bounded along the bank or leapt into the lake. But Rani wasn't after any old deer — she wanted the big stag!

"NO!" I gasped. The stag was too big. He could be dangerous!

Rani had the stag's throat in her jaws. The stag was still standing, but the tigress hung on like grim death. Shaking all over, I crept closer to grab a picture.

RANI VERSUS THE STAG

Parrots screeched and monkeys called from the forest. But the tigress and the stag were strangely silent. Neither moved – the tigress wouldn't, and the stag couldn't.

The stag freed himself with a shake of his big body, but Rani wouldn't let go. Her sharp fangs bit into the stag's leg and her clutching claws dug into his shoulder. Rani's weight pulled the stag down. But the stag was stronger than the tigress, and he dragged himself upright. The tigress dug her claws deeper into the stag's shoulder as she dodged the sharp antlers that could poke out her eyes or rip her guts.

Rani's in danger, I thought wildly, and I prayed that her wound wouldn't open up. Please, please, let Rani get out of this!

Rani pulled the stag's head down until his hind legs kicked in the air. Again the stag fought back. He shook the tigress like a kitten and shoved his heavy hoof in her face.

Raj crept through the grass to join me.

"He's killing Rani!" I gasped. "She's got to let go!"

I tried to talk to the tigress in my head. Let go, Rani. Please let go! I pleaded.

With a final effort, the stag shook himself free and ran for his life. His skin was torn and bleeding but he was alive. If a deer could tell a story – what a tale he could tell!

AND THAT'S WHEN I ESCAPED...

Rani gazed after the stag. She was panting, and her sides heaved with effort. A few moments later the cubs crept from their hiding place and tried to comfort their mum. But she turned and snarled until they backed off in terror.

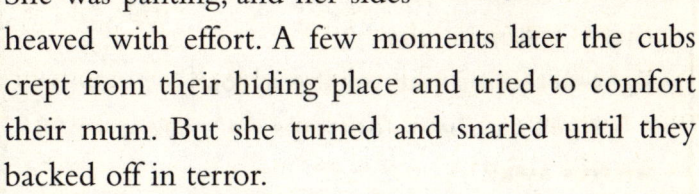

"GIVE US A BREAK!" I imagined her snapping. "MUM'S HAD A BAD DAY!"

Later

A hot, sweaty night. I tossed and turned as my mind whizzed and whirred with thoughts of the fight.

After a while, I got out of bed and looked up some facts about hunting…

TARA'S TIGER NOTES
HOW TIGERS HUNT

1. A tiger's eyesight and hearing are designed for hunting…

• Tigers aren't as good as humans at seeing colours and movement. But after dark they can see six times better than us.

Their secret weapon is a tapetum (ta-pee-tum). This is a shiny layer inside the tiger's eyeball. It reflects what little light there is onto the light-detecting part of the eyeball.

I'M RESTING MY SECRET WEAPON

• A tiger can hear footsteps on grass over 90 metres away.

2. Tigers attack from behind or from the side. Sometimes they run ahead of their prey and lurk in ambush amongst rocks or long grass. When the prey animal passes by, the tiger leaps out and pulls it down.

3. When a tiger attacks a large animal, like a sambar deer, it will go for the throat and try

> to stop the victim breathing. It kills small creatures, like wild pigs, with a bite to the back of the neck. And they can attack humans in this way...
>
> 4. Tigers don't catch anything 19 times out of 20, but hunger makes them try again. A mother tigress with hungry cubs to feed has a real job on her hands – or should that be on her "paws"? She needs to catch a deer every five to six days.

Rani may have lost her battle with the stag, but she can't give up. And that means she'll hunt tomorrow. I wonder if she'll be lucky?

March 10

Rani got lucky! We found the tigress gripping a chital deer's body in her jaws and slowly dragging it into the bushes.

"If we're careful," murmured Raj, "we can get a little closer."

I wasn't too keen on this idea. I remembered that tigers hate being bothered while they're eating. Back in January Rani hadn't exactly welcomed us with open paws. But I trust Raj, and I know that even if he's a crazy car driver, he doesn't take risks with tigers.

In the end we managed to creep close enough to see Rani eating. It wasn't a pretty sight. Even Raj screwed up his face, and he's seen more tiger meals than I've had hot dinners!

TARA'S TIGER NOTES
TIGER TABLE MANNERS

1. Tigers aren't fussy about food, They'll happily munch manky maggoty meat. In the Sunderbans area of India and Bangladesh, tigers often feast on fish, frogs and snails! And with a diet like that, you won't be surprised to learn that tigers eat earth and grass as a digestion aid for their tiger tummies.

TIGER TREATS!

2. Tigers are hearty eaters. They'll happily scoff 5 to 10 kg of meat in a single sitting. And a horribly hungry tiger will wolf down (er – shouldn't that be "tiger" down?) 30 kg of meat in a night.

3. Tiger mums usually let their cubs eat first. This is different to lions, where the adults eat first and the cubs get the leftovers.

WANT TO SWAP MUMS?

But if a male tiger's around, he'll grab the meat and eat his fill first. And there are no arguments!

4. Tiger teeth and tongues are ideal for eating meat...

- **A tiger's rough tongue licks away hair and skin. It can even lick the hair off your head – if the tiger doesn't bite the whole head off first!**
- **Incisor (in-size-or) teeth (the large teeth at the front) rip away skin from the meat.**
- **Sharp, biting – or canine – teeth tear holes in a deer's leathery skin.**
- **Side teeth slice up meat like scissors.**

5. The only things tigers can't do is chew or suck. A hundred years ago people believed that a tiger sucks blood like a stripy vampire. But that's impossible!

When Raj read my notes, he pointed out something I'd missed. A matter of life and death...

"You need to say something about the dangers of hunting," he urged. "Deer antlers and hooves can badly hurt a tiger. So can lots of other creatures..."

And with that Raj reeled off a list of tiger enemies.

SIX CREATURES TIGERS SHOULD BEWARE OF...

1. Rhinos. Bad-tempered. Too heavily armoured to attack. Tigers catch baby rhinos, but they have to beware of angry rhino mums.

WE CAN BE ANGRY MUMS!

2. Elephants. Same as rhinos. Most tigers avoid rhinos and elephants.

3. Porcupines. Stab tigers with their prickly quills. A brave tiger can kill a porcupine by biting the spiky creature's head.

4. Wild boars. Tigers fear the boars' bad temper, killer tusks, and fearsome fighting skills.

5. Poisonous cobras. Tigers are scared of snakes and rarely catch even non-poisonous snakes such as pythons.

6. Wild dogs. These creatures are the most deadly hunters in India. A tiger can deal with one wild dog but a pack of them can kill a tiger. Wise tigers hide from wild dogs.

NICE DOGGIE!

March 14

Today we watched tiger-cub playtime. Like some human games, this tiger game started with the cubs acting tough.

"I'LL GET YOU, SKINNY-RIBS!" Prince seemed to hiss.

"NO, I'LL GET YOU FIRST, STRIPY-PANTS!" Twiggy seemed to snarl back.

Well, that was too much for Prince. He chased Twiggy around in circles until she lay on her back and begged to give in. Prince is bigger and stronger than his sister now, and he enjoys putting her in her place.

You're a bully! I told Prince in my head. If I had a brother, I wouldn't put up with that!

And I'm thrilled to say Twiggy didn't either!

Suddenly the little cub leapt to her feet and whacked her brother's nose. I felt like cheering!

IT'S PLAYTIME!

Twiggy darted towards a bush with her brother at her heels. As she grabbed a branch, he tugged her tail with his teeth. Twiggy fell over, twisting and rolling. But not for long! In the blink of an eye, the two little tigers were on their hind legs with their paws spread. It was a tiger boxing match as each cub tried to whack the other.

We enjoyed a laugh trying to guess who would win. I think it was a draw! And afterwards I asked Raj why the cubs are always playing…

TARA'S TIGER NOTES
TIGER-CUB TRAINING

1. In their games tiger cubs practise vital skills they will need when they're grown up: how to sneak up on their prey, how to leap on their prey, and how to fight.

2. Tiger-cub games are rough, and boy tigers play rougher than girls.

3. When the cubs are about six months old, their mum starts to take them hunting. She lets the cubs watch and learn how to catch deer and other animals. In their second year, she'll let them hunt on their own.

We watched the cubs until Rani called them with a quiet cough. The tiger mum was in a good mood. She lay on her side and treated the cubs to a feed of milk. And so the day ended happily for the tigers ... and the tiger-watchers!

March 16

The forest is changing before our eyes. Last week the leaves on the sal trees fell in rustling, golden showers, and now shiny, new, copper-red leaves are sprouting from the bare twigs. And the flame of the forest trees are living up to their name as they burst into fiery, red-orange flowers.

I love it here, of course, but I do feel a bit ratty in the heat. Every day is hotter than the last. The midday sun burns out of a glaring sky like a brain-blasting blowtorch. Every morning I have to tie my hair back and slap on my sunscreen. And I have to wear a hat to shade my face from the scorching sun.

ME FEELING HOT!

But today the hat played a starring part in a mini-drama with mini-creatures. It happened as Raj and I were following Rani's pug marks through some bushes. I was so busy trying not to trip over the roots that I didn't notice the ball of stuck-together leaves that hung from a branch.

The ball was twice the size of my fist and glued together with gunky, gooey white stuff. It was an ants' nest. And as I brushed past it, the ant army poured out to defend their home. I never even noticed!

BEWARE!

"You'd better take off your hat!" warned Raj.

I looked at Raj in surprise. He whipped off my hat and threw it to the ground.

"Do you mind!" I snapped.

But the hat was alive with ants. Bad-tempered, biting ants. A few of their friends began to explore the back of my neck. Their bites felt like red-hot needles sticking into my flesh.

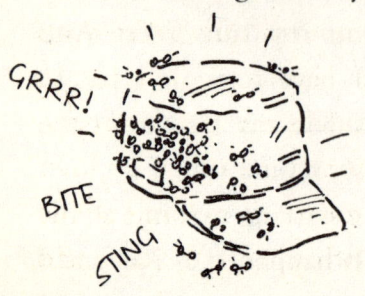

GRRR! BITE STING

"OWWWWW!" I cried, rubbing my poor sore neck. Then I saw my hat. It was jumping with ants and I felt glad it wasn't on my head!

March 17

Five pm by Rajbagh Lake. Raj said we should call it a day. The tigers had just splashed out of the water. They'd spent the day cooling off in the lake while we sat in the jeep and fried. I waved away another annoying fly and looked forward to a shower and a change of clothes.

All at once a loud bellow rang across the water. A sambar deer was in trouble! SPLASH! The big beast fell over as it fought a crowd of crocodiles. Soon a horde of hungry crocodiles was snapping at the deer's body.

Rani heard the commotion and raised her big stripy head. Hmm – what's going on? she seemed to think. She set off with the cubs trotting at her heels to find out what the fuss was about.

When Rani saw the crocodiles and the dead deer, she tiptoed into the muddy water to take a closer look. The crocodiles were too busy nipping at the deer and snapping at each other to spot Rani, and the tigress fancied a free meal. Suddenly, fearlessly, she dashed towards the deer. Whoosh! Watery spray splashed and frogs leapt clear of her big, wet paws. When Rani reached the deer, she snarled at the crocodiles. Most of them slipped away, but the biggest brute of all clung on to the body.

Angrily, Rani whacked the water that came up to her big stripy shoulders.

"IT'S MINE, REPTILE-FEATURES!" I imagined her growling. "LET GO! MY TEETH ARE BIGGER THAN YOURS!"

Rani grabbed the deer by the neck. For a moment it looked like an animal tug of war between the tigress and the crocodile. But the crocodile let go. Maybe it was scared of Rani! Well, who wouldn't be? Grimly, Rani began to drag the heavy body towards the bank.

RANI GRABS THE DEER

Meanwhile the cubs were prancing and dancing with excitement. Tigers don't just hunt for food, they steal it. For a tiger, a dinner is dinner. And it doesn't matter how they come by it!

Later

My mind is in a whirl. Something terrible has happened! Soon after I got back from the park, Mani hammered on my door. I knew something was wrong.

"Please to come quick!" yelled Mani. "The hospital is talking on the telephone. There is bad news of Mr Kumar!"

The news hit me like a bash on the head. It took a moment for Mani's words to sink in.

"Raj in hospital?" I stammered. "What's happened?!"

In answer, Mani tugged at my sleeve. "Please to come most urgently, straightaway! Mr Kumar is in car crash. It is most serious!"

A car crash? No! I thought desperately. This isn't happening. This has got to be some dreadful dream!

"Hurry!" cried Mani, running ahead over the lawn. "Mr Kumar is hurt. Maybe he is already dead!"

TIGERS IN TROUBLE

March 18

I woke up this morning feeling shaken and stirred. Much the same way as I fell asleep last night. Yesterday I spent four horrible hours in the hospital. First, I waited for someone to tell me where Raj was. Next I waited to hear how he was, and last I waited for someone to take me to him.

The hospital was hot and crowded and busy. The ceiling fans only stirred the warm air in the high, bare rooms. When at last a young doctor arrived to take me to Raj, I felt like a worn-out rag. But Raj looked worse than I felt. His hair glistened with sweat. His leg was wrapped in bandages and strapped up and hoisted in the air by a kind of pulley. Raj has broken his leg in the car crash.

"It's not a bad break," said the doctor, trying to comfort me. "But he'll have to stay here for two or three weeks."

"What happened, Raj?" I cried.

The tiger expert shook his head. "Not good," he moaned. "I'm so stupid, I'm sorry."

"Sorry?" I gasped in surprise. "What have you got to be sorry about?"

"Driving too fast," said Raj miserably. "The other guy was trying to overtake me. But I lost control. It's my fault, I guess. The jeep's a write-off."

"Never mind the jeep – how are you?" I asked.

Raj smiled weakly. "OK, the painkillers are taking the worst of the pain. And I've got my poetry book."

"I'm so sorry!" I burst out. There were tears in my eyes and I bit my knuckles.

Raj smiled. "Hey, don't worry, Tara! I'll be fine. I'm sure they'll look after me here. The trouble is, I'm in no fit state to go tiger-watching. And it could be months before my leg's completely better."

I hadn't thought about Twiggy, but as soon as Raj spoke about tiger-watching I longed to see my cub again. "Isn't there any way we could do it?" I begged.

Raj sucked in his breath as his leg gave him a nasty blast of pain and grimly shook his head.

So here I am, gazing glumly at the garden. And I'm wondering if I'll ever see Twiggy again.

March 19

This morning I arrived at the hospital to find Raj scratching his beard and rubbing his eyes. "Bad night," he yawned. "But I think I'm starting to mend. Oh, are these for me?"

I nodded, handing him a big bunch of bananas and some flowers.

Raj smiled tiredly. "I've some good news for you. I spoke to the park director, and he's promised to let you visit the park with Govinder Singh, my forest-ranger friend."

"Wow – that's great!" I cried, clapping my hands.

"You'll only get two visits a week, and there won't be much time for tiger-watching, but it's better than nothing."

It certainly is! At least I've got some hope of seeing the cubs... Thank you, Raj!

March 22

Last night I had a strange dream. I dreamt I saw a big tiger. The colours of its coat seemed to glow in the dark – orange and yellow and white. But the tiger was in trouble. A mob of monkeys were throwing stones at it. The stones thudded and thumped on the poor tiger, making it roar with pain.

"STOP IT!" I tried to scream. "Leave the tiger alone!" But nothing came out of my mouth.

And here's the strange thing. The tiger didn't run off or attack the monkeys as you might think. It slowly vanished, fading before my very eyes! First to go were its ears and tail. Then its paws and whiskers and stripes slid away like shadows. And last of all the tiger's head faded, leaving only its shiny golden eyes.

I woke up, hot and panting with the morning sun pouring through my windows and the monkeys practising ballroom dancing on my roof. I scratched my head as my mind puzzled over the dream. I believe in dreams – I think they mean something. So what is this dream all about?

March 23

Govinder Singh is a very polite, softly spoken man of about 60. He doesn't say much, but everything he says is carefully thought out. We get on really well!

Today we found pug marks around Padam Lake and I thought Rani and the cubs must be hiding in the long grass. But Govinder told me gently that his job didn't allow him to wait for tigers to appear. He had to check on the tourists and stop people taking their cattle into the park. The cattle munch the plants the deer need to live on.

No tigers today, I thought sadly as we drove back along the main road. But just then I caught sight of a stripy shape slinking along a ruined wall.

Govinder stopped the jeep and we stared at the tiger. I was sure it was Akbar! I picked up my binoculars and, yes, I was right! For five minutes we watched in delight as the big male tiger prowled along the wall. The setting sun made his beautiful stripy coat glow and I took this wonderful piccy...

AKBAR IN THE RUINS

March 26

Govinder halted his jeep to let some people cross the dusty road below the fortress.

"These people are going to puja – worship at the temple in the fortress," he said. "They have to be careful because there can be trouble with the tigers. They must keep a look-out for danger."

This evening I told Raj about the people going to the temple and the danger from tigers. We ended up chatting about humans and tigers. We talked and talked for two hours. We talked for so long that the nurse told me sternly that Mr Kumar needed his rest.

As I was leaving, Raj thanked me for the bananas (I'd brought him a second bunch) and asked me to say something about humans and tigers in my diary.

"Look on it as homework," he smiled. "You're a teacher, after all, and we owe it to the tigers to tell the whole story. Everyone must know that tigers are in danger."

Well, Raj, here's my homework. I hope it gets an "A" grade!

The sad story of humans and tigers

Once upon a time, more than 2,000 years ago, tigers roamed Asia from the snows of Siberia to the islands of Indonesia. And people held tigers in fear and awe.

But powerful people wanted to hunt tigers. They wanted to kill tigers to show how powerful they were. And so the emperors of India and the maharajahs of Jaipur killed tigers with the help of armies of servants and dozens of elephants.

In Victorian times the British ruled India and they took up tiger-hunting in a big way. In those days all tigers were seen as cattle killers and man-eaters, and the government paid hunters to shoot them.

After India became an independent country in 1947, things went from bad to worse. Hunters and farmers killed hundreds of tigers with guns and traps and poison. Only a few tiger experts pleaded with the government to stop the killing while there were still tigers left to save.

At last the government listened to the tiger experts. They banned people from killing tigers – but by then the tigers were clinging on by their claw-tips. There were no tigers left in almost all of India's forests.

The government set aside land in Ranthambhore and elsewhere, where tigers could live in safety. And all over the world children tried to help the tigers in their new homes by painting pictures and raising money. But even today – even in the national parks – tigers aren't safe. People are destroying the forests where tigers live and driving away the deer that tigers need to eat. Without food and shelter, the tigers are doomed to die out in the wild. And poachers are secretly killing tigers and selling their bodies to rich, greedy people who don't care whether tigers live or die.

I laid down my pen and a big tear dripped on my diary. I imagined Ranthambhore in the future. A future when the peaceful lakes and ancient fortress walls no longer echo to the tiger's roar. How sad and empty, how boring and dull it would be!

So that's what my dream was about! The monkeys

throwing stones weren't monkeys – they were us humans! And the tiger disappeared because that's what we're doing to tigers. Making them disappear for ever!

And I'm feeling sad for another reason. My job with Wildwatch is ending and I have to leave Ranthambhore next week. It's going to be hard to say goodbye to my friends. I'm sure I belong here and my little hut feels like home. But at least I've got a few tiger-watching days left to enjoy. And I'm going to make the most of every minute!

March 28

Disaster struck at 10 am this morning when Mani banged on my door. I let him in. The poor boy was wild-eyed, almost shaking.

"Mani, what's wrong?" I asked.

"You've been bestest pal to me!" Mani burst out.

It's true. I've even helped him with his English. (I enjoyed doing a bit of teaching!)

"I have very big secret to tell," Mani babbled. "Important man is staying in hotel. He is wearing white suit, and much jewellery. He is Mr Khan and he is talking to a man I know!"

"Slow down, Mani! What's this big secret?"

"Mr Khan is tiger-skin dealer!" Mani whispered.

I gasped in horror. Was this the man people were talking about? A sudden thought struck me. "Mani," I asked, "how do you know all this?"

Mani looked sheepish and hung his head. "I wasn't listening at the door. Not very much. But I see Mukesh Bashira. I know he is up to no good. He is bad-tempered man, most unliked in my village. Mukesh say he is going to leave poison dead buffalo to kill tigress near fortress. Mr Khan give him cash. Mukesh say he bring tigress skin and bones."

The room whirled until I felt sick in my belly. I put my hands on Mani's shoulders.

"NO!" I cried. "It can't happen! When did you hear all this, Mani?"

Mani's dark eyes filled with tears. "Yesterday evening!" He sniffed. "You weren't there. I had to go home. I didn't know who to tell."

I nearly said a rude swear word. Yesterday evening I'd been visiting Raj. What if Mukesh had already put down the poison? The tigers could be rolling around in agony! There was no time to lose. I had to do something – fast. And I was very, very frightened...

THE VALLEY OF DEATH

March 29

Last night I didn't finish telling you what happened after Mani told me about the skin-dealer.

This is all happening too quickly, I panicked. What could I possibly do? Then I remembered Govinder was coming! I felt a rush of relief. Of course! Govinder had promised to take me on another drive and he would be here at any moment!

We ran to the road and looked for Govinder's jeep. I paced up and down, worried that he might have forgotten. Then at last he appeared! I rushed into the road waving my arms. I'm not sure what I told him, but it was enough.

Govinder knew what to do. "Get in," he said. "We must go to the park at once and get help."

Quickly, I scrambled into the jeep.

"You too," Govinder told Mani. "You can tell me what you heard on the way."

Mani stammered out his story as we raced towards the park.

"Mani, where did Mukesh say he'd leave the poisoned buffalo?" I asked.

Mani was crouching in the back of the jeep. He screwed up his eyes and he tried to remember. "It's a long valley – one end closer to fortress!" he burst out.

"That sounds like the Kachida Valley!" said Govinder grimly.

Within the hour Govinder had five rangers and a second jeep ready to search for the poisoned buffalo. The jeeps screeched to a halt in a cloud of dust on the Kachida Valley track.

"We'll search the valley," said Govinder. "Miss Tara and Mani, you stay here and keep close to the jeeps. It may be dangerous."

Govinder split the rangers into two groups and they all headed into the silent forest.

Mani and I stood awkwardly by the jeeps. Mani looked scared and he kept biting his lip.

"Can you remember anything else? Anything at all?" I asked him.

The boy smacked his hand against his forehead.

"Er, Mukesh say he will leave buffalo at the lake end … of … valley."

Something clicked in my brain. That doesn't sound right, I thought desperately. What was it? Think, Tara, think!

"Mani, you said it was the fortress end!" I burst out.

"Yes, the lake end is closest to fortress!"

I gasped. A valley with a lake at the end closest to the fortress – it had to be … Of course! The *Lakarda* Valley. We were looking in the wrong place! But what could I do? It might take ages to fetch the rangers. And meanwhile the tigers might be just about to eat the poison! If I took a jeep I could go there now. I knew the area – it was near Raj's hide – and it was only a few minutes away. I told Mani my plan.

"Go and tell the men," I said. "Tell them where I've gone. Hurry up – be quick!"

As Mani ran off along the valley, I started Govinder's jeep and raced off towards the bumpy track that led to the Lakarda Valley.

As I rattled along, my brain whizzed into overdrive. I decided to park the jeep near Raj's hide. The jeep would be well hidden in the thick forest.

"You need to look for the buffalo on foot," I told myself. "You don't want the poacher finding the jeep and looking for you!"

I ran the jeep off the road and leapt out. The forest was quiet except for the busy buzz of insects. Bright sunlight shone through the gaps in the trees to make splashes and puddles of light on the dusty grass. I began to feel hot. Stinging sweat trickled down my forehead.

Breathlessly I picked my way among the old shady trees, clinging on to branches, scrambling over the rocks and roots. If Mukesh had left the buffalo here, he had chosen the spot well. It was not far from the track, but no one could see what he was up to.

As I made my way deeper into the forest, I peered around the tree trunks. The buffalo must be close by – but where? Ah, there it was! A big body, half-hidden in the bushes. I stopped and stared at the buffalo. It was starting to stink in the heat and flies buzzed around. A magpie fluttered down to perch on the buffalo's shoulder and snap at the flies. All was silent, except for a monkey family playing in a nearby tree.

And that's when I heard the sound. It was a tiny sigh. The weak whisper of rubbing, rustling leaves. All at once the monkeys began to bark their alarm calls. My tiger sense buzzed a warning. The hairs tickled on the back of my neck like an electric shock. I knew couldn't leave the buffalo. So I stood still, feeling as fearful as a baby deer. And I felt terribly alone.

I could hear my fast breathing … and the sound. The stealthy sound of something moving closer. Something like a tiger. I glimpsed stripes among the leaves, a golden-brown nose, a pair of amber eyes. It was Rani, and she had seen me! My mouth was suddenly bone dry.

Softly, softly, Rani padded closer Her amber eyes stared at me. I could see the round black dots at the centre of her eyeballs. Rani opened her jaws to show me the sharp, white killing points of her teeth. Her eyes narrowed in fury – she was less than a tiger's leap away.

I'm going to die! I thought. I'm going to die in one minute. My heart was bashing against my ribs. Every nerve screamed RUN! But somehow I forced myself to stand still. I felt the tigress glaring at me. I could hear what she was thinking as surely as if I heard her voice.

"BACK OFF!" she snarled. "MY CUBS ARE HUNGRY AND THAT'S MY BUFFALO. GO AND FIND YOUR OWN!"

I could hear the cubs crying out for buffalo meat. And now I was talking in my head. If only Rani could understand me, I could save her life.

But I can't back off, I moaned. The buffalo is poisoned!

And maybe, just maybe Rani got my message. With a disgusted huff, she turned her head aside. It's too hot to fight! she seemed to growl. But next time, beware. I might get really angry!

Rani growled again as she prowled past me. As she slunk into the shadows, I caught a glimpse of the cubs at her heels. I stood stock-still with the sweat pouring down the back of my neck. I clasped my sweaty hands to stop them shaking.

Then something moved behind me. I felt it was Rani. Was she just about to leap? Just about to sink her terrible jaws into my neck? Slowly, fearfully, I turned around. And that's when I saw the man holding a knife and heard his snarling voice.

"Who are you?" he demanded.

It was Mukesh Bashira. He was younger than I expected, a thin but tough-looking man in a black T-shirt. His hair was brushed back and his dark eyes blazed with rage. I knew that he could kill me in this secret place. And no one was around to save me...

My heart sank into my boots, but my brain, still racing from the face-off with Rani, had a plan ready.

"My name isn't important," I snapped. "I know who you are, Mukesh Bashira, and I know what you're up to!"

Mukesh's eyes widened and he gasped. "You know – how?"

"Mr Khan told me," I said coldly.

Mukesh looked at me wildly. He lowered the knife a little. "What do you know about Mr Khan?" he hissed.

"Plenty," I said, trying to sound angry. "You see I am Mr Khan's customer. You're killing that tigress for me!"

"You're lying!" snarled Mukesh, raising the knife again.

I gritted my teeth. Act, Tara. Make something up! screamed my brain. Keep him talking!

"Why else would I be here?" I said, pretending to sound annoyed. "I've come to tell you I've changed my mind. I don't want that tigress."

"What?" cried Mukesh. "Mr Khan and I have a deal. I am poor man with family. I lost expensive trap. Someone found it so I had to kill valuable buffalo."

I shook my head and shrugged. "Oh, the buffalo," I said, trying to sound like a selfish rich girl, the sort of girl who would buy a tiger skin. "What does that matter? I have plenty of money! How much do you want for your stinking buffalo? Name your price!"

Mukesh lowered the knife and his eyes narrowed. And just then I heard voices. Figures dashed towards us shouting "Mukesh Bashira!" and something in Hindi.

Mukesh whirled around. He dropped the knife and ran off into the forest with two rangers after him. I stared at the knife in the long grass. I've won, I thought wearily… I've saved the tigers!

"Are you, OK?" asked Govinder.

I looked at him stupidly. "Yes, fine," I said in a tiny little voice. And I burst into tears.

March 30

I've spent much of the past two days at the police station answering questions. But it's been worth the effort. Mukesh was caught soon after he ran away and his poisoned buffalo has been destroyed. Mr Khan has been arrested. Now he's sitting in a cell and sweating in his white suit. I can't say I feel sorry for him.

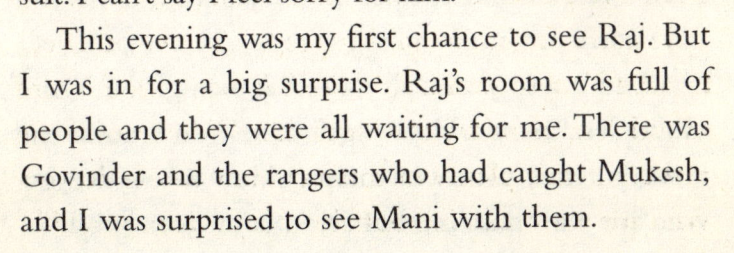

This evening was my first chance to see Raj. But I was in for a big surprise. Raj's room was full of people and they were all waiting for me. There was Govinder and the rangers who had caught Mukesh, and I was surprised to see Mani with them.

Raj was grinning up at me from his hospital bed. "The rangers wanted to say thank you," he said.

"Er – it was nothing," I stammered.

"It was brave and it was well done," said Govinder. "You are a most daring lady!"

He took my hand and pressed a one-rupee coin into its palm.

"For us in Rajasthan, it is the highest honour we can give," he smiled.

Mani clapped his hands. "Hooray!" he cheered. "The rupee is more than well earned, Miss Tara!"

WOW!

"And here is a rupee coin for you too, Mani," declared Govinder. "You are a very brave boy!"

Mani gazed wide-eyed at the small coin in his hand.

"I also have something for you, Tara," said Raj. "It's a title – *Bagh Sevak*, meaning servant of the tiger. I've been a servant of the tiger for 20 years and now you have earned the title, too."

"And we would all like to thank you," said Govinder. "In two days I will drive you around the park, but this time you may choose where we go. And we will most certainly find your tiger cubs!"

Everyone looked at me, expecting a speech. I felt myself go red as I nervously cleared my throat.

"Over the last few months," I began, "I have learnt to love India and all her animals. Especially the tigers! Thank you for helping to save the tigers, and thank you for saving me too!"

Everyone clapped and shouted "BRAVO!" and I blushed even more. Then we sat around Raj's bed and told and re-told the story of how we caught the poacher, until the nurse told us it was time to go home.

April 2

Today was my very last chance to see Twiggy. True to his promise, Govinder drove me into the park and around the lakes. But we didn't see any tigers. We checked everywhere. Nothing. As I peered into the trees looking for a stripy tiger, I wondered if I'd get to say goodbye to Twiggy after all. I began to lose heart. Where are the tigers? I asked myself for the umpteenth time. But suddenly my luck changed.

"Quick! Stop the jeep!" I shouted to Govinder.

Govinder halted the jeep and I pointed to an orange blob by Padam Lake. I looked through my binoculars. It was Rani! She stood on a strip of land that stuck into the lake and gazed at the upside-down Rani reflected in the water. All around her, the lake was covered in lovely white lily flowers.

A few moments later Rani stretched and yawned. She was just about to leave when two playful young tigers bounded from the bushes to rub noses. They were the picture of a happy tiger family. I felt a big bubble of pride swelling up inside! If it weren't for me, they would be dead.

SO LONG, TWIGGY!

But all too soon, the tigers turned and padded off into the bushes. I pulled out my hankie and waved it and called goodbye to them. And then, just like magic, they were gone!

April 3

Yesterday I said goodbye to Raj. I'm not very good at goodbyes and my heart felt heavy. Raj is my tiger teacher and I've learnt so much from him. And today there were more goodbyes as I left Sawai Madhopur station. Govinder and Mani came to the station to see me off. As the train began to move, I waved to Govinder and blew Mani a kiss as he ran alongside my carriage.

"I am hoping you are coming again soon!" yelled Mani.

"I hope so too!" I called back.

I sat back in my seat and dabbed away a tear. I thought of all that had happened in the past three months. It's certainly been an adventure — if only I could have stayed!

TARA'S TIGER LETTERS

September 25

Crack open a bottle of red ink! This morning I got not one but *two* letters from India. I opened the first and stared in amazement. It was from ... Twiggy! And here it is:

> Dear Tara,
> How are you? I am well, but I've had a hard time! The monsoon rains came and the deer headed for high ground. We followed them across fast-flooding streams and steep, muddy hillsides. Prince kept sliding down on his bottom, but somehow we all made it.
>
> The deer were hard to catch because they bunched into big herds that ran away when we turned up. We were often hungry, but Mum kept us going.

Prince and I have grown much bigger since you last saw us. I'm as long from my nose to my tail as you are from your head to your toes! But sadly me and my brother have fallen out. At night we no longer snuggle together with our heads on each other's paws. It's all Prince's fault! He plays too rough and it's more like fighting. Typical boy! At least the forest is full of bugs and frogs for me to play with.

I've seen your friend Raj a few times. His leg is better and he says that he and your friends are missing you and wondering when you're coming back to see them.

Yours tigerishly,
Twiggy

PS I nearly caught a peacock today - but Prince scared it off!

I laughed when I read the letter because I guessed that Raj had written it. Then I opened my second envelope from India…

Dear Miss Bennett,

Re: Field Worker post

Regarding your interview for the job of Field Worker for the Tiger Protection Fund based in Delhi, we are pleased to inform you that your application has been successful.

Your employment will start on 1 November and a copy of the contract will be sent to you in the next few days. Please ring or email Mrs Ambika Patel, Personnel Manager, with any further questions and to discuss when you might be able to arrive in India.

We look forward to welcoming you as a member of our team.

Yours sincerely,
J.K. Panwar (Director)

When I read this letter I punched the air and shouted "YES!" at the top of my voice. I can't wait to tell Raj. The first thing I'll do is visit Ranthambhore and see my friends, and that includes Twiggy and her family! But this time I've got a cause to fight for – the battle to save tigers from skin-dealers and poachers. If there's one thing I've learnt, it's that humans are far more deadly than tigers!

Looking back, I'm sure the fortune-teller was right. My future really does lie in faraway India. And last night I dreamt of a magical forest of tigers with eyes that burned like the setting sun. I knew it meant something and now I know what that is … it means soon I'll be talking to tigers again!

IF YOU ENJOYED **TALKING TO TIGERS**, WHY NOT TRY THESE OTHER EXCITING **WILD LIVES** STORIES BY **NICK ARNOLD**...

...**THEY'RE IN THE SHOPS NOW!**